POETRY

GREAT MINDS

Your World...Your Future...YOUR WORDS

From Norfolk

Edited by Lynsey Hawkins

 Young**Writers**

First published in Great Britain in 2005 by:
Young Writers
Remus House
Coltsfoot Drive
Peterborough
PE2 9JX
Telephone: 01733 890066
Website: www.youngwriters.co.uk

SB ISBN 1 84460 719 4

Foreword

This year, the Young Writers' 'Great Minds' competition proudly presents a showcase of the best poetic talent selected from over 40,000 up-and-coming writers nationwide.

Young Writers was established in 1991 to promote the reading and writing of poetry within schools and to the youth of today. Our books nurture and inspire confidence in the ability of young writers and provide a snapshot of poems written in schools and at home by budding poets of the future.

The thought, effort, imagination and hard work put into each poem impressed us all and the task of selecting poems was a difficult but nevertheless enjoyable experience.

We hope you are as pleased as we are with the final selection and that you and your family continue to be entertained with *Great Minds From Norfolk* for many years to come.

Contents

Travis Malloy (12)	65
Tara Shannon (13)	66
Matthew Tyrrell (13)	66
Imogen Stevenson (12)	67
Charlotte Fisher (12)	67
Shonrae Atwell (12)	68
Zoe Rawlins (12)	68
Louise Stagg (13)	69
Samantha Daniels (12)	69
Eleanor Baker (12)	70
Ryan O'Sullivan (12)	70
Megan Page (12)	71
Bethany Weyer (12)	71
Thomas Hunt (12)	72
Jazz Abbott (12)	72
Emma Hayward (12)	73
Chris Hardwick (12)	73
Tamás Dalmay (12)	74
Kelly Sweryda (13)	74
Polly Tarrant (12)	75
Holly Faber (12)	75
Casey-Lee Ralph (13)	76
Sam Betlem (12)	76
Jack Salisbury (12)	77
Alex Short (12)	77
Colette Dexter (12)	78
Stephanie Hailey (12)	78
Guy Walker (13)	79
Adam Buffin (12)	79
Rebecca Jermy (12)	80
Lucy Garstka (12)	80
Jamie Isaac (12)	81
Ben Cooke (12)	82
Bella McKinnon-Evans (12)	82
Lauren Bream (12)	83
Alex Gray (12)	83
Sam O'Neill (12)	84
Harriet Campbell (12)	84
Milly Bartlett (12)	85
Ryan Hayward (12)	85
Andrea Ratcliff (12)	86
Amy Batch (13)	86

Sam Cooper (13)	87
Aaron Hayward (12)	87
Shaun Woodward (12)	88
Matt Molloy (13)	88
Tara Cassim (12)	89
Ross Mullineux (12)	89
Justin Pryce (12)	90
Florence Brown (12)	91
Sean Messenger (12)	92
Rhys Margitson (12)	93

John Grant School For Children With
Severe Learning Difficulties

Stephen Moore	93
Michael Thorogood (13)	94
Paul Hickman	94
Naomi Sayer	94
Mark Grimmer	94

Lynn Grove VA High School

Amy Tovell (13)	95
Sarah Kelf (13)	95
Kelsey Janisch (13)	95
Thomas Parker (13)	96
Katie Fuller (13)	96
Sam Lawson (13)	96
Emily Howgate (12)	97
Jason Fowler (13)	97
Emma Wells (13)	98
Jessica Turrell (13)	98
Sarah Turner (13)	98
Sara Bone (13)	99
Daniel Snowling (13)	99
Andrew Hemp (13)	99
Paris Holmes (13)	100
William Beevor (14)	100
Thomas Dunn (13)	100
Emma Redfern (12)	101
Liam Newson (12)	102
Ian Smith (12)	102
Rebecca Bowles (12)	103

Reepham High School

The Clare Special School

Thomas Docwra (13)   189
Gary Cowell (15)   190
Felicity Stafford-Allan (15)   190
Jesca Hindley & Daisy Murwira (13)   191

Wymondham High School
Matthew Rudling (15)   191
Rachel Nichols (14)   192
Hanna Puggaard Witt (14)   193
Emily Spinks (14)   194
Megan Long (14)   194
Josh Smith (14)   195
Emma Williams (14)   196
Hannah Adcock (14)   197
Alastair White (14)   198
Lucy Spinks (14)   198
Ben Shackleton (14)   199
Olivia Jones (14)   200
Megan King (14)   201
Emma Knivett (14)   202
Hannah Lane (14)   203

The Poems

Hockey

Squashed between the sticks,
The hockey ball
Rolls on unseen
Dodging the brown sticks,
Fast   quick
Rapid   swift
Brisk   speedy
     Smash
      Goal
Hurried   noisy
Loud   blaring
Deafening   ear-splitting
     Smash
      Goal
      Win!

Hannah Day (12)

Heavenly Music

Scales, arpeggios, intervals, chords.
Music floats gracefully through the room
like a swan swimming on a summer's day.
Off the wall the sound echoes back,
the voice of our ancestors, our makers, our creators.
To feel the music is to live it. It reflects our lives
crescendoing up gradually to that all important climax
then slowly fading away. Away to that point of no return
where all is quiet, thoughtful, peaceful,
where we ascend to a better place,
where life is, but not how we know it.
It's time to let go and see another side of life.

Emma Wood (16)
Attleborough High School

Ignored

Outcast,
Leper,
I feel ignored
Part of the wallpaper
You sit and talk
Don't even realise I'm there
I could sit and cry
You wouldn't even notice
You're supposed to care
I'm treated differently
But why?
I don't understand
Am I not good enough for you?
On my own once again
I can't trust anyone.

Disregarded
Overlooked
I feel ignored
Lonely cloud in the sky
Everyone turns a blind eye
Look at me
Don't turn away
I am here
Why don't you notice me?
Used to be so close
What happened?
On my own again
I can't trust anyone.

Emma Daynes (14)
Attleborough High School

What I Feel

Not every day is bright and cheerful
As I've found out some can be rather tearful
When I was younger I found life a blast
But now I realise that happiness does not last.

The world around me continues to grow
But sometimes life seems to go very slow
All I want is to see a brighter day
And every day I pray and pray.

Inside I feel nothing but darkness
And now this day I must confess
My life is going down the drain
And in my heart I get a hard, sharp pain.

To you right now I have to admit
I'm wasting away bit by bit
My parents don't want me here anymore
And now I feel like walking out of the door.

My friends they stick by me every day
They make me happy in every way
Sometimes my friends aren't enough
Especially when things at home get really tough.

I need to hold on to a little bit of hope
Sometimes I feel I just can't cope.

Why is this happening?
Why aren't I smiling?
Why am I sad?
My life is very bad.

Somebody please help me.

Laura Jude (13)
Attleborough High School

School!

Every year a new term begins,
Children come to a new year of school,
First timers look worried and scared,
Children have brand new stationery.

The first break time of the year starts,
Children everywhere in the playground,
Everybody eating their break,
The bell goes, they go to their lessons.

The teachers call for quiet now,
The children get out their books and pens,
Another lesson has begun,
The teachers teach and the children learn.

The last lesson has finished now,
The teacher says they can pack away,
The school bell goes, the children leave,
The mums and dads are waiting outside.

Rebecca Wright (11)
Attleborough High School

Someone Is Coming

Mum came in early one morn.
When I heard the news, a tear filled my eye.
What shall I do?
What shall I say?
Will this affect me in any way?

9 months passed, my mum had gone.
Next thing I knew,
My dream had come true.
She is gorgeous,
Out of this world,
She is my sister
And more than I deserve!

I love you Hallie.

Ashlie Snelling (13)
Attleborough High School

The Magical Lunch Box

I walk into the lunch hall
With a light feeling in my bag,
I sit down at a table
And call over my pals.

Starting to get hungry,
Pull the empty lunch box from my books,
Think of what I want
And open up the zip.

I pull out chocolate ice cream,
Pull out a cream-filled cake,
It moves towards my gaping mouth,
And fills my mouth with taste.

When I get home from school that day,
I ask my mum for food,
She says no so I go upstairs
And have a little feast.

Joshua Buck (12)
Attleborough High School

Hello Stranger

Hello Stranger
I stand there numb
Waiting and wondering
If I'll remember your face.

Hello Stranger
I sense you are in the room
You're moving towards me
The crowds are parting.

Hello Stranger
You smile at me
I smile back
You're no stranger now.

Alison Winser (14)
Attleborough High School

Boredom

I'm sitting here in French
I'd rather watch paint dry
If I get more bored
I think I'm gonna die.

I'm sitting here in English
The teacher's blabbing on
I'm bored and wasting away
Now my feet have gone.

I'm sitting here in maths
The teacher's doing sums
I've been doing so much work
I've got blisters on my thumb.

I'm sitting here in art
Trying to draw a cloud
I'm fed up of sitting
So can I stand up now?

Paul Leech (12)
Attleborough High School

Life At School

Life at school is sometimes fun,
It's been years since I've begun.
Times have been really easy,
Times have also been really hard.
It's like lessons have run my life,
Some teachers are sharp as a knife.
From English, maths and technology,
To science, art and geography.
Making friends every year,
Even enemies I cannot bear.
School may sometimes be a bore,
But where would I be without school?

Sian Duval (14)
Attleborough High School

Win Or Lose

L osing all the time
I gor Biscan misses every shot
V ladimir Smicer is always injured
E very game a lose or a draw
R afael Benetez sorts them out
P lease win a game Liverpool
O h no, not again
O h yes!
L iverpool have won a game!

Daniel Skipper (12)
Attleborough High School

My First Ski

Crunchy snow surrounds my boots,
The bright sun shines on my face,
The air is like a fridge.

The snow is white like a sheet,
The sky is baby-blue,
My skis, black like midnight.

Trekking up and down long slopes,
Jumping onto quick chairlifts,
Down the steep piste once more.

Everyone having good times,
Skiing as fast as lightning,
Times on the wild side!

Again the day is over,
Oh, what fun times I've had!
Times I'll never forget,
On my first ski!

Gemma Adams (12)
Attleborough High School

Ken Bigley

K ept in prison
E xecuted mercilessly
Killed u N fairly

Missed B y his family
I mpossible to save
A G ood man
Too Late to be saved
E ven Blair couldn't save him
onlY trying to help.

Matthew Jordan (12)
Attleborough High School

My Dream

My shoes squelching and scraping
Tap, tap, tapping on the polished steps
Shouting, pounding in my ears
Brighter and glittering, lights shining.
My hands caress the guitar,
Glistening eyes fixated like glue.

The plectrum grasped in my hand
My grip tightening, not letting it slip
Sweat forming on my smooth palms
Electricity running through my veins
My hand is raised, it dives it strikes,
The loud twang echoes as the crowd cheers.

Tap, tap, tapping on the polished steps
I play as my hero walks on stage
The world's best guitarist, Slash.
As the night comes to an end tears fall,
Sparkling like precious diamonds.
The curtains fall, my eyes creep open, morning.

Whitney McKernan (12)
Attleborough High School

Dreams

Nice dreams
Nasty dreams
Ones that make you scared.

Nightmares
Falling down the stairs
Making you jump
Run back up
You're back in bed
Very, very scared.

Megan Greening (12)
Attleborough High School

The Hurricane

The wind sounded hard and threatening,
Howling at all doors,
Loudly screaming and screeching,
Making every house shake.

Here it came knocking at more doors,
Bashing and bashing,
Sounding determined as ever,
And right in it came.

Whipping up everyone's papers,
Rocking everybody's house,
Furniture flying everywhere,
Cars were flying too.

Everything that came within reach
Was instantly destroyed,
Everything was wrecked,
And not the smallest thing survived.

And when it had calmed down,
Everything was damaged,
Not only houses had been destroyed,
But also people too.

Amy Webb (12)
Attleborough High School

The New Car

The phone rang shrilly
As I entered the room,
Wanting my attention,
I answered,
Out came a booming voice,
Loud and crystal clear.

Like a wave, joy rushed over me,
A euphoric feeling
I've never felt before,
Down went the phone.
Like an elephant I clumsily danced
Round the house.

Then the next day,
Out I peeped,
Out of the window,
Onto the street,
There lay a shiny, black Mini!
With a Union Jack top glinting in the sun.

I leaped as gracefully as a gazelle,
Inside the car,
There I sat staring
At the wheel,
Put the key in the ignition,
It purred.

I drove into town,
Sitting proudly,
Watching people as I passed,
They all stopped and stared at me,
Mouths open in amazement,
Looking at my gorgeous car.

Lauren Smith (13)
Attleborough High School

My Life . . .

I believed that I was dreaming
The colours were so dim
My silent shoes were steering me
Further into the maze
Until they suddenly stopped dead.

The door handle sneaked in my hand
To lead me through the door
The delicately engraved plate
Flashed before watching eyes
But when I looked back it sprinted.

There they all sat dead still
Sitting on two blood-red sofas
All wearing suits and skirts
I watched all their saddened faces
All with blank expressions.

Then suddenly the floor gave way
Down and down I fell
I got up slowly at the end
And looked all around
Everything around was pitch-black.

I quietly started walking forward
Then suddenly I saw
Two strange lights racing towards me
Then suddenly a bang
I went up and flew through the air

Then landed on the rock hard floor
The thing that I could see
Was a midnight-black raging sky
So little did I know
That was the very last thing I saw.

Chloe Lyall (12)
Attleborough High School

A Golden Retriever Pup

I walked towards the silent door,
I heard a very quick noise.
My heart beat like a big drum,
As I was excited.

I opened up the creaking door,
Something stared back at me.
I saw two beady bright brown eyes,
Like two shining marbles.

It wore a red silky ribbon,
As smooth as a cherry.
Golden yellow, like the bright sun,
A tiny fluffy ball.

I heard a very loud scratching noise,
Like an infected cut.
I could hear the puppy scratching
The carpet in the hall.

The soft, sweet scent of doggyness
Wafted around the room.
The sweet scent of a puppy's breath
Swirled out of its nostrils.

The puppy's fur was very soft,
Its ears were very smooth.
The touch of the puppy's wet nose,
Moist, spongy, black as night.

The puppy looked around the room
For a big, juicy bone.
It went into the back garden,
And found a squeaky ball.

Sophie Moore (13)
Attleborough High School

A Dream Come True . . .

I get home, go in the garage,
Before my very eyes I see,
A car, the fastest car in the world.
It stares at me with a gloomy bumper.

Get in the shiny leathery clean seat,
Shut the door carefully
The keys are in the ignition.
Turn the key subtly and drive off.
Down the main road as if there is no tomorrow
Thank God the cops aren't around to bust me.

Go out of town - get back in late,
Want to get back in the beast.
Get in, have a beer and go to sleep
When I wake up I can't wait.
Get in the garage.

I am astutely horrified as,
The car has disappeared.
As I am sulking,
Think, *get a grip and get on with life.*
Think, *maybe life is going to be OK.*
Give up all hope of the precious car.

Wake up,
Get up from bed,
Find my feet,
Go to get my car,
To my astonishment,
A car I dreamt about the other night has arrived.

Robert Maas (12)
Attleborough High School

My Old Granada

My old slick black Granada
It's my dream to get it back
It sat there like a monster
Gobbling up all the darkness.

If I got it back today
I'd do it up real good
I'd get black tinted windows
To shut out shining light.

There'd be a big black spoiler
On the side red dancing flames
Front and rear low bumpers
And side skirts as low as ants.

There'd be pulse flashing neon
Beaming spotlights on the front
I'd have a slick black interior
Leather seats as soft as snow.

I'd buy Yokohama wheels
And beastly shiny alloys
I'd have a polar roof scoop
And a lightweight body kit.

A Celica style custom hood
As smart as a dressed up man
2 cans of Nos in the seat next to me
For that extra speed burst!

Tom Venables (12)
Attleborough High School

The Mountain

M   assive rocks above everything
O   verlooks everything
just   U   nder the clouds it lurks
there is   N   o mountain bigger
T   owering higher than anything
it burns   A   live with strength
I   t pokes its head through the skies
N   o one can match its power . . .

Stevie Hughes (12)
Attleborough High School

Melon

The slice of melon
Floats towards my open mouth
Sumptuous candy pink
The green field on the horizon
Covering the child's pale skin
Dripping with its mellow juice.

It enters the cave
As lonely as a hillside goat
Its juice drips on my tongue
Its sweet and delicious flavour
Flows down my throat tickling my taste buds
Fireworks fly inside me.

Again and again
It enters my mouth smaller still
Than before until now
It's gone forever disappeared
Apart from the end the long green field
Left on its own its body gone.

Georgie Edwards (13)
Attleborough High School

Lemon Cheesecake

The chocolate lamp post lured me ever closer
Willing for me to eat it
The milky rich chocolate melted round my lips
Tasting like vanilla fudge.

I was drowning in a sea of chocolate
As it thawed round my feet
Chocolate as hard as rock raining as hail
And I began to eat.

The constant smell of chocolate pulled me in
It made my hunger grow
The taste so delicious as it soothed my mouth
Lusciously exquisite.

I saw the many colours of chocolate
Milky white, brown and black
The spectacular colours burned my eyes
Lots and lots of chocolate.

I bring this dream to an end by saying,
'Mmmmmmm, chocolate!'

Adam Beck (12)
Attleborough High School

I Can't!

I can't write a poem to save my life,
I find it dull and boring.
Trying to write a poem is causing me strife
And it nearly always sends me snoring.

Oh please, please help,
What can I do?
I need some inspiration,
Or else I'll eat my shoe,
And will become fatally ill.

Naomi Foster (12)
Attleborough High School

Victory

Glory, glory I have to win,
Winning, winning I love to win,
Champagne and victory taste so sweet,
Crowd clapping like a thousand soldiers marching.

Glory, glory I have to win,
Winning, winning I love to win,
The crowd go wild like a hurricane,
The photographer takes a very quick picture.

Glory, glory I have to win,
Winning, winning I love to win,
Snowy white, golden yellow sparks flying everywhere,
Our feelings flood the pitch,
Our minds run wild like an antelope,
Leaping, running around the pitch,
We have done it!

Jamie Garwood (12)
Attleborough High School

If I Could I Would!

The heavy oak door invited me in,
My eyes gleamed up in excitement,
There, a coil ready to spring!

Sad eyes drooped waiting to know its fate,
Marrow-flavoured breath smelt close by,
Lush fur like a fresh-cut pitch!

Swoop from the tail hit like a twister,
Shiny nose dipped in water,
Rolling over for tickles!

My happiness spilled over like champagne,
Bubble burst, it was just a dream,
Another day with my dog!

Hannah Ewing (12)
Attleborough High School

That One Night

I'm a burning, blazing fire,
I'll spread as much as I like,
I'm always here at any time,
A fresh day or a gloomy night.

Not afraid of the tallest heights,
I'll extend into the clouds,
Big Ben is nothing to me,
I will burn it just like that.

Vibrant orange one fire colour,
Brilliant red another,
Sunny yellow, it's not like that,
My light is scorching bright.

Though I can be warm and calming,
In your homes on cold, dark nights,
You'll sit by me and read your books,
The one night I'll be your friend.

Amy Williams (12)
Attleborough High School

Worry

Worry was there watching me in the dark watching, waiting,
Worry was there talking to me making me worry even more,
My nightmare's shaking me, breaking me,
Worry was every minute of my life,
Worry was there stalking me, making me cry, making me die,
Worry kept me in a cell, trapped me,
Telling me I would never leave,
Worry was there telling me nothing would go right,
I was kept there, nowhere to go, no one to see,
No one would understand where I have been,
Worry is something no one else can see,
No one understands where I have been, only me.

Kelsey Davis (11)
Attleborough High School

Father Christmas

Early in the morning,
The white snow lay like a brand new top,
And the clear blue sky floated as if it'd never been touched,
The snow slept flat and undisturbed,
All was silent and then I heard
Light little bells miles away

Getting louder and louder
I then could see
A crystal clean sleight
Nine brown reindeer
And a fat man dressed in red.

Then I thought
Could it be?
And yes it was
Father Christmas
Then he said with a chuckle,
'Dear I missed your house!'

Laura Daynes
Attleborough High School

I Own Liverpool FC

I saw the red of Liverpool
It was such a gorgeous red
I think I saw a trophy too
It was as shiny as gold crystals.

I also heard a bombing noise
It was those marvellous fans
I smelt the luscious grass
It was like a roast dinner.

All I tasted was the hot dogs
They were as smooth as clean glass
The stands were as big as England
And as colourful as a rainbow.

James Hawkins (12)
Attleborough High School

If I Had A Dream

I lie here on the wooden spit,
My skin flaking bit by bit,
I lie listening to the chopping sound,
The knife goes up and the knife goes down.

My subtle perfume
Drifts around the room,
Like light fills the air,
I lie lazily on the spit, roasting everywhere.

Now I lie here on a plate,
Getting more nervous as I wait,
The gravy is flowing,
I lie here knowing
I'm going to be eaten
I have been beaten.

The way I live confuses me,
Humans serve me alongside peas,
Yorkshire puddings and potatoes too,
That is what they like to do.

My nerves flood the room,
I feel the moment of doom,
If only I could still run free,
If I had a dream that's what it would be!

James Chapman (12)
Attleborough High School

The Graveyard

In the graveyard dark as night,
The spooks are out, they cause a fright.
I hear a really creepy sound,
It makes my heart pound.
Look left, look right, anyone there?
Behind, in front, as we walk with care.
Don't step in the graves, beware,
My grandma's over there!

Molly Naldrett (11)
Attleborough High School

Winning The Lottery

I hear the numbers called out loud,
And then I feel on top of the world,
Nothing matters anymore,
Except all the things that I adore.

I think of all the things I want,
I could have them all - but think about
All the people who have nothing,
Could I help all them with my money?

I reach for the phone and I hear
My mum loud and cheering right in my ear,
I run fast upstairs with the phone,
So excited that I fall over.

I'm shaking now I hold the phone
I dial in my dad's home number,
As it rings I think of all the
Possibilities lying ahead.

My dad answers the phone and I
Scream and jump around with super joy,
He asks what's up and then I say,
'I've won; I've won the lottery!'

Sophie Eaves (12)
Attleborough High School

Spook

He ran through the cemetery,
Something was watching him,
Following him,
He ran faster,
Heart racing,
Something grabbed him,
He tripped . . .
Woke up!

Jamie-Lee Linnitt (11)
Attleborough High School

Man On Mars

A dark landscape of nothingness,
But quicksilver moon rocks,
The taste of my rubber spacesuit,
Like antiseptic cream.

A tiny gape in my spacesuit
Was irritating me,
Like a great whirling jet engine
Was the sound it did make.

A small rare moon rock drifted now,
Directly in front of me.
In my hands I did clench it so.
And pranced around in delight.

A small rock of all clarity,
With red sparks in it too,
I scanned it again and again,
And gently placed it down.

The moon rock is small and precious,
Like a crisp emerald,
Hard and brittle - unique type,
First man on planet Mars.

Jason Edghill (12)
Attleborough High School

My Own Myth

A fierce crimson red eye pierces my room
The room then struggling to calm
My eyes then draw attention to its
My gaze averts at once
I turn now and it seems gentle
It shyly urges me aboard
Its curled bare body an ice-cold blue
And chest a pure silky gold.

Each scale pulses as a tense muscle
As smooth as a blade of ice
I then sit on armour not on scales
We then sweep into the sky
Insignificant from where I sit
As it being so apace
Each cloud dodging and leaping away
But then to confer and bow.

This intense beast is mine to control
And to its homeland we fly
An Asian place where his myth unfolds
People's beliefs come true
My beast sets light a holy sword
A samurai then comes to see
The holy thing he worships
An ancient dragon of his.

George Notley (12)
Attleborough High School

My Non-Existent Blindness

A fool I am as I linger in the paths of sanity,
Concealing within my existence,
Drowning in a jaded rim of helpless disabilities,
Sowing my footprints to the earth I cower upon
Watching olden treasures die in darkness grasping for
Their deprived light.
I believe that as I stand in a glazed window watching
Onlookers dismiss these creatures' suffering in their anguish.
I look upon the worlds below, upwards, downwards and into distances
Saving my tears for those who can shed no more.
This is my non-existent blindness.

Jacqueline Duven (12)
Attleborough High School

I Wish I Could Be The Leader Of Hell

I wish I could be the leader of Hell
I would decorate the walls with flames
As bright as the expanding sun
Cover the floors in dripping red blood
As dark as the midnight light.

I wish I could be the leader of Hell
I would make everyone bow to me
As I have given world peace
Cover the ceiling with flesh
As the skin on your bones.

I wish I could be the leader of Hell
I would make fresh flesh pie
As the dripping cream on a bun
Cover the people in oil
And burn them in Hell!

Sophie Coulstock (12)
Attleborough High School

Fly

I launched off into the evening sky,
I felt the ocean breeze,
I flapped my wings strenuously,
Swiftly starting to glide.

The horizon lured me closer,
As if to get me trapped,
I flapped with all my strength and might,
But it wasn't enough.

The evening's turn grew to a close,
Night crept sneakily in,
Determined to follow the sunlight,
Refusing to stop now.

I perched on a tree, luscious and green,
I smelt fresh coconuts,
I saw the ocean waves collapse
And flew home, lost, alone.

Eddy Taylor (12)
Attleborough High School

Gloomy Graveyard

The graveyard sends shivers down my spine,
It gives me a sick feeling inside.
As though something is telling me,
Telling me that we're all going to die.

Names of young and old,
All with a story that's been told.
Shining stones too fresh to be a memory,
Crumbling tombstones so old and forgotten.

Freshly dug grave so dark and deep,
Holding onto their memories to keep.
Now I leave the gloomy graveyard,
To go to work as a castle guard.

Rebecca Etteridge (11)
Attleborough High School

Life

Life isn't always what we want it to be,
All the pointless suffering,
The dreaded pain and final death
That we are all put through.
What's going on?
Life's not meant to be like this.
What's with all these dramatic wars?
Is there really any point?
Why can't we all just be friends
And live a happy, fun-filled life
Until the very end?
But I suppose we all live it through,
What we do is just get on with it
And hope it will all go away,
But nothing will ever happen
Without first changing *you*.

Sammy-Jo Stewart (13)
Attleborough High School

Dark And Spooky

Dark and spooky
Silence reigns
Blind as a bat
You helplessly stumble
About the graveyard.

Big rocks and stones
Plants and trees
Inhabit the yard
Then there is the dead
They live in a world of their own.

They lived in their day
But all must helplessly fall
Into the pit of death
They know not what has happened
They still can't escape from that pit.

Thomas Pont (12)
Attleborough High School

Hell

Hell is dark like the night sky,
With light only from the fire's flames.
The evil spread around everything in its path,
And swallowed up everything that entered.

I once went down to the fires of Hell,
To see what it was like.
Its smell was like molten lava,
And screams could be heard echoing down the dark corridors.

I waited, too scared to go on,
What was out there? Who was there?
I heard an iron door slam shut,
I turned around to find that I was trapped,
Trapped in Hell.

Was I going to be trapped down there for ever?
Will I be turned into darkness?
I was surrounded by golden angels singing,
I was in *Heaven!*

Stephanie Charles (12)
Attleborough High School

What Am I?

I come quietly and gently from the open sky,
I fall softly onto the wet, cold road,
I own a certain season,
For I am . . . ?

I like to be thrown and stamped on,
I melt in your warm, bare hands,
I am only dangerous and icy when I am cold,
For I am . . . ?

I am incredibly cold and frosty,
But I look plain and bland,
I and my friends and family stay on top of the trees for many days,
For I am *snow!*

Rhiannon Whyman (13)
Attleborough High School

Second Impressions Of Ben Nevis

I could hear only my relentless gasps,
As the air had become quite thin
The swirling wind whipping the sleeping Ben
And the crunching of his weathered skin.

The same freezing wind stung my nose and tongue
Like the strong menthol in cough sweets
The exquisite sensation of success
Started filtering up, through my feet.

The feeling was moving up my body
As I climbed closer to my goal
My eyes moved up from my tired black shoes
And saw a sight worth much more than gold.

The sky was the most perfect shade of blue
Like a swaying Caribbean Sea
This perfect sky was completely clear
No clouds this time to dampen me.

This was the moment I reached the summit
It was more sublime than I can say
And though it was only halfway through,
This was my most brilliant, perfect day.

Andrew Emerson (13)
Attleborough High School

Lottery

Sitting on the settee
I'm watching TV
Ticket in my hand
I hope I win a grand

My numbers come up one by one
Can't believe it, I've won
Three . . . five . . . eleven . . . twenty . . .
My family goes crazy.

Adam Flatt (13)
Attleborough High School

Football Dream Team

F ootball is a competition of teamwork
O n the volley Henry from the cross of Ljungberg
O wen scores to make it 1-1
T erry headers home, he's number one, Tresguet fights back,
    it's level
B eckham bends the free kick onto the head of Neville
A shley Cole drives forward to cross for Rooney to score a *goal!*
L izmara Betts takes his shot and deflects off Cole
L ampard scores last minute, *goal!*

Matthew Carr (11)
Attleborough High School

My Dream

I looked upon the great acid drop,
Ready to explode and jump.
I hit the snow, twisted, turned,
I flew up, Indy grabbed;

I flipped and flipped then stopped,
I weaved in and out of trees,
Then shot off with huge air;
Sledding fast, hard like never before!

I leapt in the air hard,
I was cruising for a bruising,
I went and slashed and mashed,
Well, like I really couldn't care.

I pulled up in first place,
Then I threw myself forward fast,
I crossed the line, sharp, hard,
I felt proud like never before.

The cup ran towards me,
It leapt into my arms like fire,
I could hear them cheering;
Now, I was flying for the first time . . .

Ben Allington (12)
Attleborough High School

I Knew, I Knew It Was You

When you went away,
My heart went astray,
I could not live without you.

The wind was so cold,
And I had grown so old,
I knew, I knew,
It was you.

My love so strong,
It's been with me so long,
I knew, I knew,
It was you.

Your eyes shining bright,
Through pain or through fright,
I knew, I knew,
It was you.

Your golden lips shine,
My how you're so fine,
I knew, I knew,
It was you.

But now you're slowly coming back,
My heart doth that lack,
A love for you to see.

Natalie Coe (12)
Attleborough High School

The Scary Cemetery, Or Is It?

The cemetery's all gloomy and dark,
No moon nor stars,
Not one little spark,
Only the sound of cars.

From the smallest to the tallest trees,
Blocking out the light,
I just had to seize,
The fear, the fright.

I just can't get out of my head,
What my brain thinks,
The people are dead,
My heart sinks.

It doesn't seem scary after a time,
They seem at rest,
Dying's no crime,
We must do our best.

You think it could be wild?
But not, maybe?
For the wandering child,
Or even baby.

Loving is important when we are alive,
Would be fine,
Hopefully eighty-five,
But maybe only nine.

Next time you pass, don't reject;
At the cemetery gate,
Just show respect,
Say, 'Hello mate.'

Daniel Welsby (11)
Attleborough High School

Suicide Thoughts

Suicide is black,
As black as my coffee I'm staring at, just staring.
This knife is sharp,
These tablets are round.
I'll drink myself to death.
My soul is dead but my heart keeps vibrating,
Why am I in this world? This life I'm hating,
I'm going to lie down, curled in the middle of my bed.
In the middle of this cold, isolated room.
Four walls just staring at me, closing me in,
Posters on my wall of things I want to become,
Pictures of loved ones, enjoying good times, having fun.
But bad times are what I have become, they are who I am.
Feeling down.
A slow death would be nice.
Shows how much pain I have eating away inside of me.
The sharp point of the blade piercing into my skin.
The bitter feeling,
Scarlet emotions filling up my room,
No one here to hear me shout,
Oh God help me, help me out!
I've been pushed over the edge, wound up inside,
There is nowhere at all I can hide.
What has life to offer me?

Charlie Everett (16)
Attleborough High School

Friends

F riends are like family
R esting or playing but always together
I n school or at home
E very day we're with each other
N ever-ending friendship
D ancing round with each other
S pecial friends, we're always together forever.

Laura Moore (11)
Attleborough High School

Her Evil Stepdad

A long day of school,
and it's time to come home,
so she meets her mum in the car park.

They are driving home,
and off goes Mum's phone,
so she answers it.

It's her stepdad,
who is really mad,
'Come home quick or you'll get it.'

They pull up in the drive,
'At last they've arrived.'
She's scared now of what he will do.

She opens the door,
and she's scared even more,
but she quickly runs up the stairs.

There she finds her stepdad,
who is waiting for her
in her room.

He pushes her roughly toward the sheer drop of the stairs,
but accidentally pushes her down,
she's screaming and suddenly silent.

Jessica Jackson (12)
Attleborough High School

The Things I Like

I like 'Lord of the Rings'
I dislike chicken wings
I really like football
I practice against the wall
I love chicken kebabs
I hate the science labs
Shooting guns is not nice
Bread should be sliced.

Daniel Hammond (11)
Attleborough High School

The Graveyard

As darkness fell in Norfolk,
We wanted to explore,
We've done the streets, we've done the shops,
But tonight we wanted more.

'Graveyard!' someone shouted,
So we walked towards the gate,
We'd seen it in the light of day,
But now it was quite late.

In the sky, the moon was out,
And shone upon the graves,
Normally nothing scares me,
But tonight I wasn't so brave.

The mist crept around the headstones,
We couldn't take no more,
I ran and ran and didn't stop,
Until I reached my door.

Laying in my bed that night,
I'd thought of what I'd done,
And although it was super scary,
It was also kind of fun!

Kerry Cross (11)
Attleborough High School

The Dead!

Like you are now so were they,
Like they are now we will be,
But right now we are okay,
Soon you will see,
Beneath the earth is the dead,
Waiting for another life . . .

Jade Paul (11)
Attleborough High School

How's Life?

What's it like
To live in a grave
Beneath the ground
On which we stand,
On that same ground
Where you once stood
Many a year ago?

Where it's cold and damp
And quiet and still.
Can you hear
The world above?
The voices,
The wind and the rain?

Does there lie
Below us now,
A better place
For us to go?
The answer to this
I'll one day know,
Let's hope that day
Is not today.

We must not wish
Our lives away.

Joshua Bunn (11)
Attleborough High School

Thank You

I feel happy as my life is somewhat secure,
Sleeping in a bed, having central heating, electricity,
Hot and cold water, even having a roof over my head,
We shouldn't take these for granted,
Some people don't have these privileges,
So I wrote this poem just to say thank you for these things.

Thomas Saunders (11)
Attleborough High School

Autumn

Autumn brown leaves blowing in the wind,
The summer season's come to an end.
A breezy wind blows down my neck as I watch the children playing
in the park,
The leaves fall one by one onto the ground.
People try to rake them up but more just keep on falling,
But it does look nice when they fall.
The raindrops splash onto the floor,
And the wind blows the leaves more and more.
The sun starts to shine just a little bit,
But the air is still cold and wet.
Even though summer has gone, winter will soon be here,
But enjoy the autumn weather as it will suddenly disappear.
The clouds start to gather up, as it starts to rain,
People start to run in their homes to shelter from the rain.
In the morning you walk to school,
The sky is oh so misty you can hardly see where you're walking.
The nights get earlier, everyone starts to stay inside,
Instead of going out to play they sit inside all night and day.
Hallowe'en will be here soon and you will see children dressed up,
Having fun, trick or treating.
As your mum tucks you in bed at night,
The wind outside gives you a bit of a fright.
You go in her room and climb in her bed you kiss,
Her on the cheek, you curl up and say goodnight.

Nicolle Ashby (11)
Attleborough High School

The Fantastic Me!

Me, me, glorious *me*
As tough as a nut, as smart as a bee
I was born in a package wrapped up with glee
And dancing is my fave hobby
In this poem I sound boring as you can see
But ask anyone I'm *crazy!*

Chloe Edwards (11)
Attleborough High School

Dead

The cheerless wind whistled,
Through the sinister thistles.

The lightning strikes with thunder too,
Rain starts to pour as thickly as glue.

The clock has struck midnight,
And the dead, they take flight.

The grave, it stood frozen,
The graveyard has chosen.

Who shall be their unlucky victim tonight?
This person will be in for a very big fright.

Whoever they pick will need to be brave,
This person will be killed by one from the grave.

The dead hold a grudge for this person who shall,
Be killed by this spirit who is not their pal.

The dead hold a mystery of who they can kill,
Small, thin or fat, feeble or shrill.

The lost is now slithering up on his few,
Bang! They are gone, next could be you.

Bethany Gibbs (11)
Attleborough High School

Being Me

Knowing what I want is the best way I can be
Being pushed around is something I don't see
Sometimes I'm confused, frustrated and annoyed
Not always know what to do, my mind it gets destroyed
Being happy is good and all I want to achieve
Is to lead a good life and not be deceived
For me being me is the best way I can be.

Emma Crouch (14)
Attleborough High School

My Dog Tara

I know a dog named Tara,
She really is the best,
She's the best dog in the world,
She's better than the rest.

Tara's colour is black and brown,
With white patches too,
She's cute and very cuddly,
You can tell that this is true.

Tara is a happy dog,
Every single day,
She's playful and she's perfect,
In every single way.

No other dog can take her place,
Because she's the only one,
She loves to eat her tasty treats,
But now my poem's done.

Jessica Hunter (11)
Attleborough High School

The Graveyard

So little spice,
Too many mice,
Dark at night,
It could do with some light.
The family plot,
Is the saddest of the lot,
The mother, the daughter, the father, the son,
All because of a bottle rum.
One Sunday night,
There was no light,
They sped off the road,
To dodge the toad,
And that is the way of life!

Nick Manias (11)
Attleborough High School

My Side

My sister wrote a poem in the school book,
But now I'm going to take back all she took.
The poem was mean and cruel to me,
But there's two sides to every story.

She says I'm stupid, she says I'm thick,
But why does my work just get a tick?
She says I'm an alien from a different planet,
But that's impossible, I would have a name like Janet.
She says that I shout and I scream,
But that's a sight she's never seen,
As you can see, she's the one who annoys me.

Josh Potgieter (11)
Attleborough High School

My Cat

T ough
H ealthy
A nxious
T iny

C ute
A dorable
T abby

That spells my cat.

It is tough as old boots,
Healthy as an apple,
As anxious as a rabbit,
Tiny as an adult's hand,
As cute as a cute thing,
Adorable as nothing else I have seen,
Tabby because he is.

Dominique Davidson (11)
Attleborough High School

Animals

A is for all animals, they are so cute,
B is for bears which don't eat fruit.
C is for cats, they run around and play,
D is for ducks, they swim around all day.
E is for elephants with a huge trunk,
F is for frogs, they go for a dunk.
G is for goats, they eat hay,
H is for horses, they grunt and they neigh.
I is for iguana, reptile and scaly,
J is for jackal, they hunt for food daily.
K is for kangaroo, bouncy with a pouch,
L is for lion, don't let it bite you, *ouch!*
M is for monkey, they swing through the trees,
N is for newt, swim in water with ease.
O is for octopus, legs they have many,
P is for panda, they hardly have any.
Q is for queen bee, the leader of all,
R is for rabbits, so cute and so small.
S is for snake, slide from side to side,
T is for tuna fish, they like to hide.
U is for unicorn, a mythical beast,
V is for vulture, on dead animals they feast.
W is for whale, its skin is so dull,
X is for xeme, a fork-tailed gull.
Y is for yak, a cow with long hairs,
Z is for zebra, its stripes are in pairs.

Rebecca Denney (11)
Attleborough High School

My Dog

My dog's really bubbly,
But sometimes a real mess.
On one wet day
Out in the garden,
I called him in,
And he was as black as coal.
In the morning when I got up
He was white,
As white as the ice on a frostbitten morning.
He has his breakfast,
Goes outside,
And comes in filthy.
He looks just like a cow,
I think to myself,
Bath time,
When he comes in,
God, what a sight!
Dripping, matted fur,
And the smell, you can't mistake it - wet dog.
I shooed him into the bathroom,
Heaved him into the bath,
I then rubbed the shampoo in,
That's better,
Melons,
Out came the shower,
On it went,
You hear a yelp,
The water all brown and greasy,
That's the price you have to pay,
To keep a dog.

Rachael Lane (13)
Attleborough High School

It Is Really Hard To Write A Poem!

It is really hard to write a poem,
There are so many things it could be about,
Such as flowers and fairies, happy things and sad,
Things that make you cross and others that make you mad,
Yet I have chosen to scrap all of those,
And to tell you how hard it is to write a poem.
You have to choose whether to rhyme or not,
Whether to rhyme in couplets,
Rhyming couplets can often be
Rhyme lines one and three,
Or not have any rhymes at all,
Yet I have chosen to instead of those,
Have some rhymes on some lines and some lines not to rhyme at all.
You have to describe what type of poem to write,
Such as limericks, haikus or acrostics,
But I have chosen to just write a simple poem,
Now how hard is that?

Freya Morter (11)
Attleborough High School

About Me

I am kind, I am funny,
I don't like honey.
I have a little sister,
She's a pain like a blister.
We sometimes fight,
But usually are alright.
I have a best mate,
Who thinks I'm great.
I love my new school,
Art is cool.

Gemma Ready (11)
Attleborough High School

Friends

Friends always come and go
They never seem to stick around
One day they are there
The next they are not
From school to school
We all seem to go

Friends always come and go
The sight of their big bright smiles
The sound of their quiet, squeaky voices
The smell of their strawberry shampoo
The warmth they bring within
They always seem to go

Friends always come and go
Some are kind
Some are fools
Some you miss
Some you don't
Friends always come and go.

Charlotte Cushion (14)
Attleborough High School

About My Cat

My cat Chloe is very bright,
She hasn't got terribly good sight,
She is very light.
Sometimes she brings shrews,
But never has she brought a screw.
We take her to the vet,
But she has never been a horrible pet.
She is black and white,
And doesn't usually fight.
She wouldn't dare bite,
And she cuddles me at night.

Amie Peck (12)
Attleborough High School

My Favourite Friend

You love to play,
You sit and stay.
Your favourite toy is the ball,
You always come when I call.
When I'm sad,
You make me glad.
You never ask too much of me,
You love to go to the sea.
You're always there to look after me,
When we walk we feel free.
Who am I?
My name is Sky.

Scott Hall (11)
Attleborough High School

Sadness

Sadness is a broken leg
Sadness is a pair of ruined trainers
Sadness is a lost friend
Sadness is a parent's divorce
Sadness is a child crying
Sadness is getting to the end

Sadness is moving away
Sadness is getting bullied
Sadness is no memories
Sadness is no food
Sadness is long blue tears
Sadness is something everyone is told.

Sophie Horan (11)
Attleborough High School

Christmas Dinner

Christmas is that happy, merry time of year,
When everyone's together to laugh and cheer.
Open the wine, dinner's nearly cooked,
Now I can smell it, I am hooked.
Everyone is eating soup now,
Even though I can't see how.
The big turkey is on its plate,
So now we no longer have to wait.
Yummy, yummy,
Fills my tummy.
Now that we've had our roast,
We are having toast.
Not really, it's time for Xmas pud,
I don't like it much, though I should.
So instead it's ice cream for me,
And for another twenty-three.
All the crackers are on the table,
And it's time to think of the stable.

Holly Furneaux (12)
Attleborough High School

Christmas Time

Holly and ivy on the door
Crisp snow falling on the floor
Bells are ringing
Children are singing
Stars are shining bright
Hope Santa will come tonight
Decorations hung around the room
I hope the first present is for me
Mistletoe in the hallway hang
Crackers going off with a bang.

Layla Adcock (11)
Attleborough High School

Starlight

Stars are coming out at night.

Stars are bright,
Stars are white,
Stars shine brightly like lights on the Christmas tree.

Stars are diamonds,
Stars are pearls,
When you put them on you'll shine like a light.

Stars are snowdrops,
Stars are crystals,
When you see them fall, you will feel very cold and rich.

Stars are shooting by like a silver car,
Stars are going by really fast,
If you see them you will find it very hard to keep up.

Stars are the best,
Stars are better than the rest,
You just can't get better than that,
Can you?

Laura Rutter (13)
Attleborough High School

Chocolate

I like chocolate, Cadbury's is the best,
It is especially better than the rest.
It is always filling and always there,
It is milky and brown and I eat it with care.
Every time I look at it, I always want a piece,
Sometimes I eat it for a midnight feast.
It is now all gone, I will need to buy some more,
But I've spent all my money on chocolate,
And now I'm very poor.

Hayley Briggs (11)
Attleborough High School

Competing At The World Championship!

As I watched them go in and come out,
I mounted and warmed up,
I saw the person before me come out,
I enter the ring, now I couldn't turn back.

I cantered round waiting for the bell,
We cleared jump after jump,
Her stride as ever like a soldier's,
We finished with perfect timing.

I leapt off my horse, my face shining like a star,
I was presented with a medal and a trophy,
I held the trophy high into the air,
The crowd cheered as loud as a lion's roar.

Emily Bacon (13)
Attleborough High School

Planets And Space

P is for Pluto
L is for land
A is for aliens
N is for nitrogen
E is for Earth
T is for the universe
S is for Saturn

A is for astronaut
N is for nebula
D is for dimension of the planet

S is for solar system
P is for pulsar
A is for asteroids
C is for craters
E is for equator.

Jonathan Knapp (11)
Attleborough High School

Tornado

The thing outside hurls and swirls everything around,
It rips up hedges and trees from the ground.
People run and scream for their lives,
Shops and houses, they all dive,
From the swirling, whirling thing outside.
Turning over cars and vans all over the place,
Taking them away so there's no trace.
Litter is twisted and turned round and round,
And in the end there is nothing left to be found,
From the swirling, whirling thing outside.

Bryony Lund (12)
Attleborough High School

Pink Elephants Rule!

Elephants are jolly,
Elephants are nice,
But if you buy an elephant
It will come at a price.

They leave huge piles of dung
All over the kitchen floor,
But you can't even kick one out
'Cause they don't go through the door.

But if you get a pink elephant
In a cartoon book,
He will always be house trained
And will fit in the smallest nook.

And so you see my friends,
A normal elephant might be cool,
And he might be jumbo,
But . . . *pink elephants rule!*

Ben Rickard (11)
Attleborough High School

Christmas

Christmas is my favourite time of year,
All the pretty lights and decorations hanging on the trees,
Children getting excited because they know it's near,
It's a time where we give lots of gifts and presents,
On Christmas Day me and my brother race down the stairs
to get to the living room,
And under the Christmas tree we see . . . a big stack of presents,
But we mustn't forget what Christmas is about . . .
Baby Jesus' birthday.

Abigail Matthews (11)
Attleborough High School

Dancing In America

I've been to visit America and France
At both places I went to dance
As I performed on the Walt Disney stage
I looked around and was quite amazed
To see those people with beaming smiles
Made it worthwhile to fly all those miles
And clapping hands which made me cry
I didn't want this feeling to go away.

We met Pluto and Daffy Duck
I couldn't believe my family's luck
We were standing here in their place full of magic
But soon I'd leave, and that was tragic
It was so sad waiting to depart
But Disney Land and will stay in my heart.

Aimee Cooper (11)
Attleborough High School

My Dream

The first time I set foot on a football pitch,
Playing for the team I love and have supported since I was six,
It was the roar of the crowd and the feel of the wet grass on my feet
When I set foot out of the tunnel,
The smell of the smoke from the fireworks set off by the supporters
And the sight of all the thousands of faces looking at me,
If only that was true,
I would do anything to make my dreams come true,
But if you want a dream to come true,
It is down to you, no one else.

Joe Thomas (13)
Attleborough High School

My Life

My life is like a roller coaster
Round and round, over and over
Going to school is like a chore
Maths and science are a bore.

My life is full of joy
Whether it's getting a pet or a new toy
I have some bad times
But many are good
Being with my family
Just like I should.

Overall my life is the best
But I really think it's one big test.

Natasha Keach (13)
Attleborough High School

White Christmas

I can't wait until it's Christmas!
The tip of the trees covered in soft, white, icy cold snow,
Our presents being wrapped with a small, neat, little bow,
The ice-cold, watery taste as snow hits my warm tongue,
And the sound of Christmas carols being sung.

The smell in the kitchen where hot chocolate is being made,
We think about the place where Jesus laid,
The burn of my hand as I touch the boiling hot glass of my fireplace,
I see the reflection of my face.

The sound of pitter-patter of white ice balls hitting
the cold green grass,
And later on another year will come to pass,
I also want it to snow this year,
So we can have snowball fights and beer,
But most of all I want it to be here.

Natasha Potgieter (13)
Attleborough High School

Dolphins

Waves crashing against the shore
And the squawking seagulls
The salty fresh seaside air
A perfect day for a swim with a gleaming dolphin
I can taste the wonderful air of the fresh seaside
The scent from the sea is just like the smell after it rains
A smell that is just wonderful
This certain fragrance beings back memories
Beautiful memories of when I was little playing on the beach
Now I have something else to remember
Swimming with dolphins.

Jay Foord (13)
Attleborough High School

Perfect Person

The perfect person has everything they dream,
A circle of friends all around.
The perfect figure, the perfect face,
Expensive clothes, shoes and make-up.

The perfect person has no dry skin or spots,
She has long wavy locks which flows in the wind,
Has no worry in the whole world,
Wakes up every morning bright and cheerful.

The perfect person goes in a daydream,
A click of her fingers and the dream is here,
Every day she's bubbly and bright,
But then she realises no one is perfect.

Sarah Binks (13)
Attleborough High School

The Iraq Story

A zoom in the air,
A flash of grey,
A burst of speed,
Spurting guns,
Ripping metal,
Burning flesh,
Crushing bones,
A field of blood,
Covered in shame,
The Yanks attacked us,
Not the other way round.

Alexander Thorpe (12)
Attleborough High School

Life

My life is so perfect
Not in just one way
I have everything I want
And every friend I need

But that is not the truth
Not a single bit
I feel small and unwanted
Wanting time to pass away

I just want to be loved
Just once to feel special for one day
Cuddled and kissed
Just please make me feel that way.

Bethany White (13)
Attleborough High School

Razzdus

Razzdus is my puppy,
Only six weeks old,
He is soft and fluffy,
And loves the cold,
He sounds like a walking horse as he runs around,
He sleeps like a silent angel on the ground,
He loves to play ball with the other dogs,
And he hates the fog,
He is as black as the midnight sky,
And as sweet as a chocolate bar,
My dog Razzdus.

Charlotte Stratton (13)
Attleborough High School

Smashing Mate

You're the cherry on top of my icing cake.
You're vanilla ice cream piled high upon my plate
You're a double chocolate wonderful dream
My splendid smashing mate.

You're like marshmallow in my berry shake
You're strawberry ice cream with little chocolate flakes
You're a fizzy Coca-Cola float
My splendid smashing mate.

Ashley Rivett (13)
Attleborough High School

Millionaire

I am the richest man in the world,
Yes, that's me alright,
A millionaire with style,
Money comes from the left,
Money comes from the right,
In fact money comes from all directions.

I buy, buy, buy,
Gifts, presents, treats for myself,
Even designer clothes.
But then nothing,
I've gone bankrupt.

Levi Lister (13)
Attleborough High School

I Want

I want to go to Lapland,
I've heard it's very grand,
There's lots and lots of snow,
But still I'd like to go.

I know it's very cold out there,
But I don't really care,
I'd like to ride upon a sleigh,
And throw snowballs every day.

I'd like to see a polar bear,
One that does not scare,
I know that if he sees me,
He'll eat me for his tea.

I've been to many places,
And seen lots of different faces,
But I really want to go,
Where there's lots and lots of snow.

Rebecca Norton (14)
Earlham High School

The Old Village

Scaly serpents scarping the sky
Creatures capture crystals
Hobbits hobble hideously
Ferocious fights fighting frantically
Fierce fires frightening families
Rivers rippling rather roughly
Rabbits running randomly
Creepy caves crying
Angry arguments appearing
Walking wood wildly
Wrecked wood wailed.

William Ives-Keeler (12)
Hethersett High School

The North

(Based on 'Northern Lights' by Philip Pullman)

It's cold, dark and treacherous,
Distant cries haunt you forever,
Snow stinging your ghostly face with blinding darts.

The cold can numb your mind,
Your life flashing before you,
You're trying to stay sane and positive by continuing to be awake.

The land before you is like a white velvet blanket,
Snow is falling so fast you can't see your hands,
You feel as if you're walking for evermore,
Facing a white, glistening blizzard,
Quickly becoming a nightmare.

Your wolf skin hat, coat and mittens
Are desperately trying to heat your frozen body,
Each breath is a struggle,
You feel your brain falling asleep,
Drifting away, drifting away . . .

Emily Elvin (12)
Hethersett High School

Playing Away

Lipton Rovers play Waterloo School.
Kevin has learnt a lesson today.
Football is his passion.
He has blown it.
Tantrums, selfishness.
Anger caused him to foul in the match,
Running away.
Not able to accept punishment,
His cowardly attitude caused mayhem.
It involved his parents and the police,
It made him ashamed.
He won't do it again.

Sam Arthurton (12)
Hethersett High School

A Cat's World

Padding down the hallway,
On white velvet paws,
The cat slinks out of the cat flap,
To sharpen his claws.

The smell of a bonfire,
The tweet of a bird,
Exciting things to find,
In the outside world.

He hisses at passing strangers,
He rolls in the dust,
He pounces on crawling insects,
He does what he must.

His head held up proudly,
His tail in the air,
As a puppy trots past the garden gate,
The cat gives him his meanest glare.

He yawns and he scratches,
And leaps onto walls,
Then it's back through the cat flap,
Back through the hall.

Inside the warmth,
He licks his tabby fur,
Then he curls up on an armchair,
And lets out his loudest purr.

Victoria Allen (12)
Hethersett High School

A Place

(Based on 'Holes')

The ground is dry, the air is empty, there is no atmosphere.
There are no people, there is no water, there is nothing here.
You could walk for metres, even miles, there will be nothing there.
No trees, no water, nothing at all, not a single animal hair.
There are no trees except two, but no one would dare go near them.
For that's where two yellow spotted lizards live .
If you get bitten, it doesn't matter where you go
Because there's nothing you can do to survive, nothing you can *give*.

James Holland (12)
Hethersett High School

Secrets

(Based on 'Bend It Like Beckham' by Narinder Dhami)

I have a secret I must not tell
I feel really happy but I feel really sad
I can't tell my mum or dad
And I feel really bad,
But football is my dream,
Playing with my friend in a football team.

Chelsea Marley (13)
Hethersett High School

Violence

(Inspired by 'Matilda' by Roald Dahl)

Fear of coming home as violence awaits
as I get blamed for all their mistakes including me!
Tears falling down my face as I shut myself into the only safe place.
I hear shouting as they yell through the barrier of my world.
I blank the comments.
I was unloved and dreamed of happiness, but it failed to come.
I lay in pain once more praying that my dreams will come true,
As I drift off to sleep . . .

Kirstin Tidy (13)
Hethersett High School

Mr Humpty Dumpty

Once upon a time there was an egg,
Who fell off the wall and broke his leg.
He was called Mr Humpty too,
That's why he fell off, he'd got the flu.
Mr Humpty cried and cried,
'I've fallen off, I'm terrified.
If I keep sneezing and breaking up,
We'll never win the World Cup.'

Mr Humpty thought and thought,
The king's men, that's who he brought.
He used his mobile phone,
To call old Billy Jone.
He was the mighty leader,
Who brought his big retriever.
Over the scene the men all ambled,
Then decided to have Humpty scrambled.

Megan Haney (12)
Hethersett High School

The Gates Of Evil

(Based on 'The Book of Dead Days')

Boy travelled to the edge of night,
Where the stars are all alight,
And the evil bronze gates
Covered in naked figures writhed in light.

Boy walked through the dead gates,
Which he knew created his fate,
He couldn't see what lay ahead,
Because moon had failed and the sun was dead.

Mille habet mors portas quibus exeat vita
Unam inveniam.

Helen Blyth (12)
Hethersett High School

Arctic Fox

(Based on 'Arctic Fox' by Mary Ellis)

My name is Alex and I have found a white Arctic fox.
I didn't know how she got here but my conscience was confusing me,
I had to take her back.
So against my own will we finally arrived at the Arctic.
All I could see was snow like diamonds suffocating the growth
on the hard ground.
My new friend Canny told me about his father going missing
and ending up in another country.
My conscience was tickling my brain again.
Is there a link between the two?

Siberiana Longordo (12)
Hethersett High School

The Journey With No Return

Terror shadows our faces,
Dangerous, heaving seas crash over our frail landing craft.
Unbeknown to us, our futures are doomed.
Our hearts thumping as we approach the shore.
Will we survive this bloody day?

Bullets speed through the water
Like piranhas ripping flesh from our bones.
Staggering through the bloodstained sea,
Towards the exploding beach.
Will we survive this bloody day?

Endless explosions deafen our screams,
Searing pain and fear abounds,
Mutilated bodies cover the once golden sands,
Men are falling, dying, all around.
Will we survive this bloody day?

The stench of death overcomes me,
Where there was once hope, now there is none.
A strange silence falls all over.
I did not survive that bloody day.

Dominic Wilcockson (12)
Hethersett High School

Snow White

Little Miss Snowy shone like the snow,
Her little soft face and her cheeks used to glow.
That was before the huntsman came,
And the queen cackled that she'd never see her again.
The huntsman declared that he was on a break,
And Miss Snowy was to run further than the lake.
When the queen found out she wept and wept,
And the mirror watched the queen, it peeped and peeped.
Meanwhile little Snowy skipped along to a hut that stood in the wood,
A little dwarf answered the door and little Snowy put up her hood.
'Hello, hello,' said little Snowy, 'here's 50 quid for the rent,' she said,
I will just put my case on this bed.
Little Snowy and the seven dwarves parted and she thought
                                        them rather dishy,
They sensed this and whispered and talked, they thought something
                                        was rather fishy.
She told the dwarves, 'I'm sorry, I'm not what I seem,'
And took off her pale, glowing cheek mask as she beamed.
'I tried to tell you I feel like a wreck,'
She looked up to reveal the face of Shrek!

Robyn Bull (12)
Hethersett High School

Midnight

Moon is shining, lighting up the dark,
It is eerily quiet in the park.
Danger could occur around any bend,
Night-time is the day's end.
I am snug and safe in my room,
Good protection from the gloom.
Hopefully soon, morning will come,
Then I open my curtains to see the sun.

Kelly Cartwright (12)
Hethersett High School

War

German bombs are like wailing trees
Blowing up anything they hit.
The siren sounds like a little girl crying
As if she has lost her parents in an air raid.

The wardens are as strict as German soldiers
Taking you (as a prisoner) to a concentration camp.
The food is like it's been preserved in *dirt* for 50 years
And then brought out just to eat,
Then buried in dirt again when finished.

The gas masks always steam up
When you have a drill at school,
So you feel like you're blinded by the bombs,
Although you're not.

The shelters in the back garden
Are always flooded when it rains,
They aren't that good anyway,
All they do is protect you from flying shrapnel.

But if you catch a direct hit
Somebody
Will find your bones and your teddy
Sitting fifty-five years later.
You are a ghost now!

Alex O'Connor (12)
Hethersett High School

The Ocean

The ocean is big and blue,
Something you can see right through.
Its hands reach out and grab the sand,
Clinging on to a piece of land.
It gives a wave when you walk by,
Calm, like the clouds in the sky.

Catherine Joule (12)
Hethersett High School

Roast Dinner

Sunday now what about Sunday?
Sniff, sniff
Ehh, now I remember, *roast!*

Now it's time, chicken, beef
Whatever the meat
Yuck!

Mash, bash
Whatever
Chuck it in the trash.

Roast potatoes
Yorkshire pudding
Now, why them?

Vegetables, peas, sweetcorn
Now yellow and green
Norwich City.

Roast, nooo! Toast, yes
By the way
I'm a vegetarian.

Chris Wells (12)
Hethersett High School

The Graveyard

The mist was hovering above
The graves, like a hungry kestrel
Searching for its prey.

The dark stones loomed
Like shadowy figures
Watching over the graveyard.

The swirling mist
Swirling, swirling
Could it be?
No, it couldn't be.

Nathan Wilson (12)
Hethersett High School

Jack And The Beanstalk

This story starts when one day,
Jack's mother said this in a very moody way.
'We're going to sell our cow, dear Jack,
So I can brighten up this shack!'
Jack said OK and went to get Daisy -
She was very fat and *very* lazy.
Jack walked into town and saw a man
With a pouch of coins and a frying pan.
'Would you like to buy my cow?
She'll make a very good meal for thou!'
'In return I'll give you these beans,
They'll grow big and they'll grow green.
These beans are magic - you shall see,
What a great opportunity I've given thee!'
Jack agreed and skipped home happy,
But when his mother found out, she went batty . . .
She picked up the beans and threw them out,
Then she began to shout.
'What were you thinking you stupid boy?'
This was obviously a silly ploy.
The next morning Jack woke to a big surprise -
A stalk had grown right up to the skies.
Jack ran outside to the shed,
So he could hit the witch on the head.
He got to the top then realised,
It was a giant, not a witch, who lived in the skies.
But he was too late - the giant had seen Jack,
He had no choice, he couldn't go back.
'I'm going to squish you into pulp!'
The giant then swallowed Jack in one big gulp.

Holly Wardale & Rois Deegan (12)
Hethersett High School

There Is A . . .

There is a monkey in me . ..
Playful and amusing
Jumping from tree to tree.
Rustling the treetops,
Moving about.
I hang on trees with my furry tail
Able to hold my weight.

There is a piranha in me . . .
Vicious but small
Pouncing on every chance
Swimming in a group
Eating anything that falls in our path.

Aaron Cobb (13)
Hethersett High School

Betrayal

Ninety-one men set out one day
Finding out they were led astray
Stuck in a trench, left to die
And all of them wondering why.

Their comrades falling one by one
Without a chance to fire their gun
'Save us Jesus,' the soldiers cried
While back in England the generals lied.

Ninety-one men set out one day
Finding out they were led astray
Stuck in a trench, left to die
And all of them wondering why
Why? Why? Why?

Travis Malloy (12)
Hethersett High School

The Thing

He sits alone
All day, all night
The Thing, they say
Is quite a fright
Yet none have ever dared
To see The Thing
That lingers so slowly
The Thing that weeps
And cries and mourns
The Thing that eats
Dead leaves and thorns
Who watches everyone
With rage
From tallest tree
To darkest cave
An unknown secret
Which he keeps
Is why he cries
And mourns, and weeps
To us his secret
Won't be known
The Thing shall always
Cry alone.

Tara Shannon (13)
Hethersett High School

Calm

As calm as the fluorescent blue sea
As calm as the cool air breeze
As calm as a winter morning
As calm as a running stream
As calm as a sleeping baby
And now, you are calm.

Matthew Tyrrell (13)
Hethersett High School

The Spice Of India

Sand choking me,
Surrounded by desiccated wasteland,
Isolated by the outside world,
Then it hit me hard,
Where was the spiced exotic banquet piled high?
The ladies draped in fine silks,
Gold embroidery jewels that glisten and catch eye?
There were none, *no food, no joy, no nothing.*
I passed starving, desperate faces praying,
Pleading in desperation,
Dying before my eyes,
It tore me apart,
Like pouncing wolves ripping me apart,
Enjoying every piece,
One small, innocent child dropped to the ground,
Dehydrated and frail,
I knelt at her side,
What I saw in her eyes was truly terrifying,
Then she died.
    Just think!

Imogen Stevenson (12)
Hethersett High School

English

I have been asked to write a poem,
The whole class as well; I am not alone.
My brain keeps churning on words I should know,
I think my head is about to blow.
I have checked on the Internet to see if I can cheat,
But I only found butchers who tried to sell meat.
have not started thinking on what I should do,
But let's all be honest, I haven't a clue.

Charlotte Fisher (12)
Hethersett High School

Friends

A good friend is like a computer,
I enter your life, save you in my heart,
And format your problems ,
And never delete you from my memory.

I dropped a tear in the ocean,
And when they find it
That's when I'll lose a friend like you.

Knowing a friend like you
Has made me happy in a million ways,
And if you ever have to leave
I'll find a million reasons to make you stay.

Of all the friends I've met,
You are the one I won't forget,
And if I die before you do,
I'll go to Heaven and wait there for you.

Shonrae Atwell (12)
Hethersett High School

Midnight Feast

Something rapping, something tapping,
It's coming through the door,
Something grabbing my feet,
Pulling me along the floor.

It's so grimy and slimy,
Dragging me to the shed,
I caught a sight of his face,
What a gruesome head.

Up they come, teeth so bare,
Standing next to these monstrous beasts,
Is this how it will end,
Because I'm the midnight feast.

Zoe Rawlins (12)
Hethersett High School

A Full English Breakfast

Waking up early from the smell of a full English breakfast
The smell warming your heart
Jump for joy, get downstairs quick
Dad's cooking, nearly burnt his hand
With eggs spitting in the pan
Eggs, scrambled, boiled or fried, which way?
Can't make up your mind
Bacon cooked just right or with a crispy texture
Everyone waiting, hurry up, hurry up
Tummies rumbling, mouths watering
Sausages sizzling, fried bread crisping
Toast bursting out of the toaster
Tomatoes moist, mushrooms cushiony,
Black pudding soft
Only beans to go, microwave pinged
Everything done
Everyone at the table, the smell kisses your nose
The taste fills your heart with delight
Cooking is a pain
Eating it a pleasure.

Louise Stagg (13)
Hethersett High School

My Dog Basil

My dog Basil is short and brown,
Sometimes he ends the day with a frown.
He used to be quick on his feet,
But he always likes his little treats.
He runs around with excitement,
But sometimes he can get quite frightened.
His long, sharp teeth are cleaned once a week,
For this, thank goodness, he is mild and meek.

Samantha Daniels (12)
Hethersett High School

Spring Food

In spring when the mornings are ripe
All the birds sing, doesn't matter what type.

We go out on a picnic, yummy
Find a good spot where it's nice and sunny.

Crisps, sandwiches, yoghurt and chicken
All the strawberries are ripe for picking.

Down in the valley there's a stream
All the children shout and scream.

Joyous laughter while playing with food
We are all in a pretty good mood.

Food that we shared, food that we ate
We didn't realise it was getting late.

The sun is setting, the laughter dies down
We all walk home through the town.

Sleep has come, our beds await
Passing through the garden gate.

Everyone's happy as we call round
Then we sleep without a sound.

Eleanor Baker (12)
Hethersett High School

Full English

As I wait for the sausages,
While they sizzle in the pan,
Beans are good for everyone,
So eat them up and get dessert,
If you eat those white eggs,
You'll be fit for all the day,
As you push the bread right down,
It pops up nice and brown.

Ryan O'Sullivan (12)
Hethersett High School

Restaurants

The smell of spices is so heavy you can almost taste it.
That smell draws you in like a fish caught on a line.
As you enter the restaurant the comforting warmth keeps you moving.
The waiter shows you to a seat and places a menu in your lap.
You look at the many choices and smell the food around you.
The sound of knives and forks clanking makes you want to eat
even more.
When you finally order you melt down into the squishy seat and wait.

Your meal is placed in front of you.
Your mouth waters and your taste buds scream as you scramble
for a spoon.
You place some in your mouth, it's perfect, it's wonderful, it's what
you wanted.
The texture is smooth and creamy.
And you are faced with a fusion of spices whirling round your mouth.
You feel at home in the restaurant and you feel it's too good to leave.

Megan Page (12)
Hethersett High School

Chinese Takeaway

Yummy, yummy chicken balls,
I like to eat them all,
White rice, special fried rice,
It's all very nice.

Chinese chips, sweet and sour sauce,
Prawn crackers of course,
Fortune cookies, pancake rolls,
I like to eat them all.

Jungle curry, Chinese curry,
I will be eating them in a hurry,
Crispy fried selected vegetables,
I like to eat them all!

Bethany Weyer (12)
Hethersett High School

Carrots?

Carrots, why carrots?
Apparently you can see in the dark when you eat them,
Never worked for me,
Don't know about you?
I've always been hitting my head when getting in bed.
Maybe you should eat them just before bed,
Imagine that, hey!
A slimy taste in your mouth,
It would be like cod liver oil
In the olden days,
Or maybe it's just a myth.

Thomas Hunt (12)
Hethersett High School

Food

A few baked beans on a slice of toast,
A glass of wine and a juicy roast,
A few chips with a bit of battered fish,
Some crispy lettuce in a salad dish.

A bowl of rice with some spicy curry,
And for desert a big McFlurry,
Some freshly caught fisherman's trout,
And all served up with some garden sprouts.

It all makes me feel good,
Like some Christmas pud,
When I have some Christmas cake,
I always have it with a Flake.

Jazz Abbott (12)
Hethersett High School

What I Hate

My mum likes spaghetti
My dad likes spaghetti
My brother likes spaghetti
But I *hate* spaghetti.

It is the thought of eating it
The orange slimy strings
Wiggling down my throat
Just like worms.

My mum likes Bolognese
My dad likes Bolognese
My brother likes Bolognese
But I *hate* Bolognese.

It is the thought of eating it
The lumpy mixture that it's made of
I can feel bumps going down my throat
It is disgusting.

But most of all I hate
    Spaghetti Bolognese.

Emma Hayward (12)
Hethersett High School

Pizza Football

Pizza is really like a game of football
You start by preparing your team
And then you play ball.
First of all you're running round the box,
You dive in, you pick up the ball,
You dribble it in,
And you shoot into the wide open goal mouth.

Chris Hardwick (12)
Hethersett High School

The Foods Of The Four Seasons

Foods of the winter.
Nothing feels better coming home on a cold winter evening
than being welcomed by the comforting warmth of a hot soup or stew.

Foods of the spring.
As you walk down the street, as soon as the slight breeze wafts
the smell towards your nose, your stomach begins to rumble,
and your mouth waters, for a barbecue is the most delectable feast
on a Sunday spring afternoon.

Foods of the summer.
The whole of summer can be tasted in just one sweet strawberry,
then the relief of a cool refreshing ice cream, to revive you
from the heat of summer.

Foods of autumn.
The smoky taste of bacon sums up a beautiful autumn sunset,
then the fun of cutting the festive pumpkin into Hallowe'en faces.

Tamás Dalmay (12)
Hethersett High School

Pizza

The smell is making my mouth water,
It's sitting on a plate in front of me,
It's making my taste buds tingle.
I can see slices of pepperoni,
Pieces of pineapple, chunks of chopped ham,
And best of all stringy, melted cheese.
A slice has been placed in front of me
I pick it up and take a bite.
The cheese is smooth and creamy,
It's melting in my mouth.
I love pizza.

Kelly Sweryda (13)
Hethersett High School

Mushy Pea Pie

Thursday night, mushy pea pie night.
My mum shouts upstairs, 'Tea.'
My tummy churns up inside me as I sit up at the table waiting . . .
She walks into the room, in one hand was the pie
And the other was a massive spoon ready to slop the pie on my plate.
I just sat there staring at my mushy pea pie.
It looked revolting, all green and lumpy
With the pie crust lying on the side.
My mum said to me, 'Come on, eat up.'
So I picked up my fork and poked it, it seemed OK.
I picked up a tiny piece of pie and slowly put it in my mouth.
I started chewing and then I swallowed.
I could feel the lumps falling down my throat
I quickly grabbed my drink and I drank it all,
And that was the last time I had mushy pea pie.

Polly Tarrant (12)
Hethersett High School

Cherry

Her eyes are like dark chocolate,
Lips like red cherries.

Her hands like juicy star fruit,
Hair like smooth spaghetti.

Her legs like sugared breadsticks,
Tan like toffee fudge.

Her smell like minty peppermint,
Curves like a small plum.

She makes me go
Bananas!

Holly Faber (12)
Hethersett High School

Mess At Dinner Time With My Brother Charlie

Along comes a flying knife, spoon and the fork,
Then he shouts out, 'I hate eating pork!'
Splat! On the floor goes his lovely food,
Which makes my mum in a very bad mood.
He undoes his strap and gets off his chair,
With all his food stuck in his hair.

Dinner time is over now and the mess is all cleared up,
But then he has a paddy and smashes his cup.

My mum is at her wit's end, she didn't know what to do,
But then we all remind her, he is only two.

Casey-Lee Ralph (13)
Hethersett High School

So Many Foods

There are so many foods I detest,
Like rotting cabbage oozing off my plate,
Like hot dog in paper at the school fête,
Like gooey mangoes, these I do hate.

There are so many foods I crave for,
Like chocolate bars melted in cream,
Like duck in pancake, that's what I dream,
Like banana covered in toffee ice cream.

I wonder if there are these foods
Like sausages in chocolate with a sprinkle of ghee,
Like custard and mustard poured into your tea,
Like a small cherry pie with honey from a bee.

But nothing can top
The scrumptious pop
Of popcorn in the cinema.

Sam Betlem (12)
Hethersett High School

Chips

Saturday night comes round again,
We drive to the chip shop through the wind and rain.

We stand in the queue waiting for our go,
While I wait, I watch the fish get cooked really slow.

We get our food and come out of the shop,
To find the pouring rain and wind has come to a complete stop.

I eat my chips in the car, filling up my tum,
I can only think of one word to describe chips and that is yum!

Jack Salisbury (12)
Hethersett High School

Food Fananza

Food is good
Food is nice
Crisps, chocolate
And sugar mice.

Breakfast in the morning
Tea at night
Cornflakes and milk
With a cup of Sprite.

I come home from school
Crying for food
There are no strawberries to munch on
Now I'm in a mood.

I sit down at the table
To have my lovely tea
My mum gives me this golden stuff
She says it's from a honeybee.

It's night-time now
We are eating our supper
Mum says, 'Put the kettle on
Anyone for a cuppa?'

Alex Short (12)
Hethersett High School

Delicious Desserts

Strawberries and cream, served with a spoon,
Plus a chocolate sundae if I have room.
Butterfly cakes hot out of the oven,
Strawberry tarts or chocolate chip muffins.

Cheesecakes, carrot cake or chocolate cream éclairs,
Doughnuts, chocolate pudding or candyfloss at the fair.
A slice of apple crumble or maybe four,
All this food makes me want to eat more.

Raspberry jelly wobbling over my plate,
Flans and pecan pie which I both hate.
All this food in my tummy,
So much to choose from, yummy, yummy, yummy.

Colette Dexter (12)
Hethersett High School

Anorexia

Food on my plate,
It's moving about.
I can't eat it,
I'm going to be sick.

Junk food, fatty food,
Sliding down my neck,
I'm trying to lose weight,
Why eat this?

Think when you eat your food
Someone is in the toilet,
Forcing themselves to be sick.

Getting thinner, thinner, thinner . . . shrinking,
But still I'm not thin enough.

Stephanie Hailey (12)
Hethersett High School

Spring Holidays

I used to dread spring holidays
I know it sounds quite strange
But for me it was spring cleaning for all of my days
Hoovering, dusting, it never changed
Everyone else was tanning themselves on the beach of Spain
But for me it was de-weeding the garden
Or washing the car in pain
But I knew I would harden
Because I lasted the summer holidays.

Guy Walker (13)
Hethersett High School

Ketchup

The lid of
the ketchup is
all sticky with
dried up ketchup
moulded to the lid
When you tip the bottle
upside down the watery
tomato juice falls out
onto your plate as the
lumpy red, delicious
ketchup falls out. The
bottom of the bottle is
full with ketchup stuck
onto the bottom which
has been left to mould
and does nothing
forever and ever.

Adam Buffin (12)
Hethersett High School

Week Days

Monday: steaming pasta piled on a plate,
Tuesday: rice, sweet and sour is what we ate.
Wednesday: chicken breast with sweetcorn and rice,
Thursday: layered lasagne, minced beef lightly spiced.
Friday: fish and chips with mushy peas straight from the can,
Saturday: soft, crispy pizza sprinkled with pineapple and ham.
Sunday: my favourite meal of the week is roast potatoes
and flavoursome meat.

Rebecca Jermy (12)
Hethersett High School

Days Of The Week

We always have certain meals for the days of the week
Monday is pasta
Tuesday is curry
Wednesday is chicken nuggets
Thursday is mash potato and pork chops
Friday is takeaway
Saturday is spaghetti Bolognese
Sunday is a roast.

My favourite meal is on Sunday
The meat is always sizzling hot
Either new or roast potatoes
Yorkshire pudding, gravy and veg
It always takes ages to make
But the food makes up for it
Because of its sweet taste.

There's always a good old takeaway
Chinese, pizza or my favourite chips
You can have salt, vinegar and side orders
It's always so hot, it burns my tongue on the tip.

The rest of the meals I like quite a lot
But they're my two favourites
Today is Saturday you know what meal that is . . . !

Lucy Garstka (12)
Hethersett High School

Blackberry Picking

(Dedicated to Christine)

In the summer
On a sunny day,
We pick blackberries
With you there.

We have tubs
That we put the berries in
But most of them
Go straight to the mouth.

Some are big
Some are small
Some are sweet
Some are sour
But all taste nice in Granny's jam.

It isn't easy
'Cause the bushes are prickly
And the good ones are all at the top.

Reaching high
Reaching low
Reaching through
And trying to get round
All this to get to the good ones.

At last
The tub looks like a pot of jewels
And one day this treasure
Will be spread on toast for you.

Jamie Isaac (12)
Hethersett High School

There Is Something About A Roast Dinner

Sitting round a table at Christmas with all your family,
Everyone happy,
Warm and content,
Like mice snuggled up in a ball of hay.

There is something about a roast dinner.

Thick gravy over sweet, lush green peas,
Runner beans and asparagus with melted butter over them,
Tender beef crumbling in your mouth.

There is something about a roast dinner.

Crispy brown roast potatoes,
Cauliflower and leeks covered in white sauce like snow on a hill top.

There is something about a roast dinner.

Ben Cooke (12)
Hethersett High School

Different

The meal arrives on the table,
and everyone tucks in.
Food piling into their mouths,
some dribbling down their chins.

As the waitress rushes past,
I look around and see
masses of people fat and thin,
all the various degrees of obesity.

So ugly the way they fork it in,
unaware of the effort been made,
piling their plates again and again,
the diet has been delayed.

At one crowded table,
but looking all alone,
a pale, silent, haunting figure
sits there, skin and bone.

Bella McKinnon-Evans (12)
Hethersett High School

Food Is Great

Food is hot, food is cold,
It can be something you cut or something you mould,
Everyone loves it day and night,
Just stick it in the oven under the light.

Food is something we all enjoy,
It's fun, it's tasty, it's vital too,
Salads, roasts, soup or stew,
Whatever you want, it's up to you.

Microwave dishes of all different types,
Quick tasty snacks in the middle of the night,
Burgers with onion, bangers and mash,
Big pots of steaming corned beef hash.

Eat it in a restaurant or eat it in your home,
Have it cooked for you or cook it on your own,
You need a plate, fork and a knife,
Because food's a part of everyone's life.

Lauren Bream (12)
Hethersett High School

Brownies

Brownies are a special treat,
They're really something nice to eat,
A bit of cream (ooh!) that hits the spot,
Best when they are nice and hot.

They ooze, so gooey, on the plate,
Cor, I can hardly wait,
Mum's recipe is the best,
Head and shoulders above the rest.

They're life in the cake tin is very brief,
The only downside -
They stick to you teeth,
Mmmm . . .

Alex Gray (12)
Hethersett High School

In Someone Else's Shoes

We sat down to dinner,
A fine succulent chicken dinner marinated in honey,
With lush peas and sweet swede,
With delicious potatoes soaked in gravy.

After with a warm feeling in my stomach,
I started thinking about people in poorer countries,
With a scarce amount of food,
What would it be like in someone else's shoes?

Sam O'Neill (12)
Hethersett High School

Concoction

Into the pan I put some Spam
Maybe, maybe a bit more ham.
Paprika, hot chilli and a cinnamon stick,
In goes the honey nice and thick.
Stir it up and add some juice,
And maybe a dash of chocolate mousse.
Toss in a birthday cake,
And a pot of fruity bake.
Stir it up and make it tasty,
Please don't be quite so hasty.
A pot of ice cream,
Water from a stream.
Some tuna paste,
Now time to taste.
Take a spoon and have a lick,
Urgh! Disgusting, I'm gonna be sick.
Put the concoction in the bin,
It's all been a terrible sin.
Please, please don't be a pain,
Never, ever make that again.

Harriet Campbell (12)
Hethersett High School

Swings

My hands touched the cold, hard metal
And peeled off some old, flaky paint
The soil beneath me was muddy and wet
Making a shiver go down my spine
I sat on the old, bent, black seats
Holding the creaky chains
And started to slowly swing
The rusty bolts creaked
And cracked under the strain
The smell of metal was overwhelming
But the breeze just blew it away
It seemed to talk in a silent voice
Telling me to swing harder
Childhood memories come flooding back
Like a giant wave in a silent sea
As I swing steadily higher
Almost touching the sky
I am a bird!

Milly Bartlett (12)
Hethersett High School

Hethersett Football Club

Hethersett Football Club is really great
I bet you have a laugh.

The players we've got and the coaching staff
We will thrash any old lot.

A bitterly cold winter morning
All the scarves are sold out.

All the players warm up at half-time
What about a lime not an orange.

At the end of the match we're all worn out
All the parents lend a helping hand.

Ryan Hayward (12)
Hethersett High School

Housework! Oh Housework!

Housework! Oh housework!
I hate you, you stink
I wish I could swap you for something puffy and pink
If only my family could do a bit
Housework I've had it
That's it.

Housework! Oh housework!
You're last on my list
And why do you ever exist?
You make my silver rusty
And my floors all crusty
And I won't give you another think
Housework! Oh housework!
I hate you, you stink.

Andrea Ratcliff (12)
Hethersett High School

Cliffhanger

'Don't look down,' I hear the instructor tell me.
I look up at the clear blue sky,
Then look down at the thick, gold sandy ground.
I let go of the cold, bumpy mountain
And cling onto the rope for dear life.
I feel my heart beat faster and faster,
I look down once again and pray I was down there.
I hear whistling past my face and I shiver.
Slowly slipping down I feel my heart beating faster and faster,
once again.
I'm getting nearer and nearer to the lovely sandy gold ground.
'Don't let go!' I hear again.
I wont let go,
I can't let go!

Amy Batch (13)
Hethersett High School

Haiku Dream

My mind leaps forward
On wings of glowing starlight
Hunting little dreams

My mind catches dreams
On lines woven from wisdom
And reels them inside

A camera twists round
Snapping possibilities
For my resting eye

Logic is shattered
By my rampaging ideas
Pieces falling away

All is possible
Imagination runs wild
In the seas of sleep.

Sam Cooper (13)
Hethersett High School

Power Cut

The trees have caused a power cut
No hot water or cups of tea
And no lights on for you and me.

There's a power cut, no hot food or TV
Because there's no electricity on
For you and me.

Aaron Hayward (12)
Hethersett High School

Place Of Mystery

Mazes of twisting canals and alleyways
Place of mystery and . . .
Each building embellished in its own conspicuous style.
Competing with its neighbour,
A short walk could take you
Four centuries ago.
Each corner leading to
Another surprise.

It might be a market seller shouting,
Or a church looming,
Over everything else.
Every shop decorated with extreme talent,
Their window frames carefully carved by hand,
Each of their engraved patterns different.

It is a museum,
Or yet one that has been transformed.
The pink light of dusk,
Romantic.
The perfect place to be . . .
Venice!

Shaun Woodward (12)
Hethersett High School

Poems

P oems can be rude, funny or glad,
O thers are disturbing, boring or sad.
E very poem has a rhyme,
M ost poems pass the time.

Matt Molloy (13)
Hethersett High School

A Black Person's Story

She has beautiful black velvety skin,
With hair in long, shiny braids,
She is very tall, nearly touching the sky,
And has a big attitude too with it,
She tries to make friends, trying so hard,
But people hate her,
But she doesn't care,
She's powerful!
John-John sings a song,
A racial song,
A song that makes her heart bleed,
But she doesn't let anyone see this pain,
'Maleeka, Maleeka, she's so black we can't even see her.'
That's his song,
See it's mean, isn't it?
So there is a point to this poem,
It doesn't matter if you're different on the outside,
We're all the same at heart,
But at the end of the day,
She's always OK,
Because she is loved by her mum!

Tara Cassim (12)
Hethersett High School

Asterix

There's Asterix and Obelix and Son
It took almost all of their fun
But they didn't know
The baby would have to go
When Cleopatra turned out to be the mum.

Ross Mullineux (12)
Hethersett High School

Jack And The Beanstalk With A Twist From His Mother's Point Of View

I sent my son out to sell our cow,
But he brought back some beans.
I don't know why, I don't know how,
But I wasn't very keen.
So I chucked them out the window as far as I could throw,
And suddenly among the weeds they started to grow.
The stalk grew so high, fat and tall,
Within seconds it was higher than the garden wall.
So I shouted at Jack,
'What type of bean is that?'
So Jack climbed the beanstalk very high,
After a few minutes he was near the sky.
He was so high I could not see,
So I went inside for a cup of tea.

Half an hour went by,
And then from the sky,
Two people slid down at fast speeds,
And Jack was first sliding into the weeds.
As quick as a flash,
He got a chainsaw and started to bash,
The stalk was as hard as could be,
For there was a giant coming down who would eat him he would,
But before he could yell,
The beanstalk fell.

Jack's body was found
10 feet underground.

Justin Pryce (12)
Hethersett High School

Ha Ha Pink Sheep

Ha ha pink sheep you haven't any wool,
Not even a purse, never mind a sack full,
You're bald and you're cold,
And you shiver in the rain,
Ha ha pink sheep, all alone again.

Baa baa black sheep why do you laugh so?
It isn't my fault that I shiver in the snow,
My fur isn't thick,
And a jumper I can't make,
But please be my friend,
Or my heart will break.

Ha ha pink sheep, guilt I do not feel,
You haven't got feelings, they just aren't real,
You have no friends,
You are funny looking too,
Because you aren't beautiful,
Poke fun I have to do.

Baa baa black sheep why do you hurt me so?
It isn't my fault that my fur won't grow,
I have tried many potions,
It is filling me with woe,
But please be my friend,
Or I will have to go.

Sorry, sorry pink sheep, I'm starting to feel bad,
I am so sorry that I made you feel sad,
You can be my friend,
You are beautiful too,
Everyone is different,
Black, pink, white or blue.

Florence Brown (12)
Hethersett High School

Twister

It spins
Like a
Spinning
Tortoise
Spinning
Spinning and
Spinning and
Spinning
It spins
And
Spinning
And
Eventually
Sucks
You
Up
Into
The
Centre of
The
Twister
And
Then
It
Comes
To
A
Stop.

Sean Messenger (12)
Hethersett High School

The Mummy's Tale

Long, pointed bodies
With a stump head
Bumpy but smooth
The sunlight shines
On their polished
Chestnut heads
Dark red demon eyes
Soft and gently pulsing
They may seem
Waiting for their
Victims to fall into
Their trap.
They love the smell
Of human flesh and blood
Of heads and toes
Just like where they come from.
Gives you the shivers.
They lived inside the
Remains of the Egyptian Mummy
Absorbing his ancient spirit
That is waiting for revenge
On all mankind.

Rhys Margitson (12)
Hethersett High School

Football

I like to play football
Mum takes me to the field and I kick the ball
I score goals
I wear football boots
I get very muddy
I support Norwich
I have been to Carrow Road to watch them.

Stephen Moore
John Grant School For Children With Severe Learning Difficulties

The Book

I like the book about a bus
Because it drives along the road
It takes people to the city
Where they do their shopping
Then they come home on the bus.

Michael Thorogood (13)
John Grant School For Children With Severe Learning Difficulties

Walking

I like to walk on the beach with Jenny
I like to walk up town and walk to Argos
Walking is good for me
I like walking better than using my wheelchair
I don't like walking in the rain.

Paul Hickman
John Grant School For Children With Severe Learning Difficulties

Church

I go to church on Sunday
I go in my wheelchair
Daddy, Mummy and Josh go to church
We sing songs in church.

Naomi Sayer
John Grant School For Children With Severe Learning Difficulties

Playing Football

I like being a goalkeeper
Save the ball when it comes
Kicking the ball high in the air
Cos that is what goalkeepers have to do in football.

Mark Grimmer
John Grant School For Children With Severe Learning Difficulties

Happiness

Happiness is bright yellow
Happiness tastes like chocolate and candy and smells like flowers
Happiness looks like a smile on your face
Happiness sounds like your laughter
It feels like sunshine on a rainy day.

Amy Tovell (13)
Lynn Grove VA High School

Love

Love is full of warm colours - pink, red and yellow.
It tastes like chocolate Aero bubbling in your mouth.
Love smells like the perfume he bought you for your birthday last year.
It looks like joy, happiness and smiles all around.
Love sounds like his heartbeat beating in your ear.
It makes you feel like a butterfly flying free in the air.

Sarah Kelf (13)
Lynn Grove VA High School

Jealousy

Jealousy is a dark, miserable shade of green.
It tastes of strong bitter lemons
And smells damp, sour and disgusting.
Jealousy looks painful and sickening
And sounds like chilling screams.
Jealousy is envious, frustrating and very irritating.

Kelsey Janisch (13)
Lynn Grove VA High School

Hate

Hate is a black dullness
It tastes like a fruit without flavour
And it smells like a dank, mouldy corner of an unused house.
Hate is a dark shadow that follows you around wherever you go.
Hate is the sound of nothing.
   Hate hates me!

Thomas Parker (13)
Lynn Grove VA High School

Loneliness

Loneliness is colourless
It tastes like plain water
And smells like a foggy morning
Loneliness looks like an empty field
The sound of echoing laughter
Loneliness makes me go cold.

Katie Fuller (13)
Lynn Grove VA High School

Freedom

Freedom is green grass
Freedom tastes of sprinting across the beach
It smells like peace
It looks like a crowd cheering and chanting together
Freedom feels like you are unstoppable
It sounds like a breeze blowing through your hair
Freedom is sunlight.

Sam Lawson (13)
Lynn Grove VA High School

Puppies

We hear them yap, as we look through the bars.
We see them stare at us with chocolate-brown eyes.
We watch them catch the ball we've thrown.
We watch them roll about in the mud.
The puppies, the puppies,
How cutely they roll.
The puppies, the puppies,
Wake you early on a Saturday morning.
We watch them chase a small cricket.
We watch them stare at a small cat.
Sooner or later,
They will be chasing that cat,
With a smile from ear to ear.
And that shoe we once lost,
We will find in the puppies' basket.
The puppies, the puppies,
Little devils in cute coats.
But the puppies will always be there,
When you're upset,
When you're happy,
And
When you need a good friend by your side,
The puppies will be there.

Emily Howgate (12)
Lynn Grove VA High School

Peace

Peace is crystal-white
It tastes like smooth vanilla ice cream
It smells like a cold, fresh winter air
Peace looks like a cloudless sky
And sounds like freedom
Peace feels like the cold air in your face
Peace is unstoppable.

Jason Fowler (13)
Lynn Grove VA High School

Happiness

Happiness is yellow and bright.
Happiness is the fresh taste of whipped ice cream.
Happiness smells like the pure summer's breeze.
Happiness looks like the glowing blaze from the sun.
Happiness is the sound of playing children.
Happiness is friendship.

Emma Wells (13)
Lynn Grove VA High School

Loneliness

Loneliness is grey and dull.
It tastes like bitter lemons and smells of isolation.
Loneliness is a dream that's drifted out the window.
It sounds silent as if the world has died.
Loneliness is forsaken friendship.

Jessica Turrell (13)
Lynn Grove VA High School

Loneliness

Loneliness is white
It tastes so plain and dry
And smells like melting plastic
Loneliness looks like a never-ending path
It sounds like dead trees swinging helplessly
Loneliness feels blunt and offensive.

Sarah Turner (13)
Lynn Grove VA High School

Love

Love is soft pink,
It tastes like chocolate heaven,
Love smells like strawberries and cream,
Love looks like a field of fresh flowers,
It sounds like butterflies flapping,
Love feels free and warm.

Sara Bone (13)
Lynn Grove VA High School

Curtains

In all rooms these floating curses
are blowing back and forth.
Blocking light, attaining darkness
reaching out to me.
The different patterns, different colours
each are far more sinister.

Daniel Snowling (13)
Lynn Grove VA High School

Darkness

Darkness is black
Creeping up on your back
Darkness is swift and silent
Never stopping
Roams through the streets like a deadly mist
No one knows where it goes
Creeping up on innocent souls.

Andrew Hemp (13)
Lynn Grove VA High School

What Is Love?

Love is sensational and glowing
Its pure radiance dazzles you
It tastes sweet and delightful
But also comes the sounds of laughs and cries
You laugh because you've found it
But yet you cry because you're so scared that it will all go away
Love looks like nothing you have seen before
Because you seem to be the only person alive
It's out of your world and further than the universe.

Paris Holmes (13)
Lynn Grove VA High School

Death

Death is black,
It tastes like a sour lemon.
The smell is of rotting leaves and dead earth.
It looks like a frozen path.
The silence stays unbroken.
Death feels final . . .

William Beevor (14)
Lynn Grove VA High School

Peace

Peace is the colour of the icy crystals in the snow gleaming
in the sunshine, freshly laid in a bitter cold morning.
Peace is the freedom to taste anything,
it would smell like the green meadow being cut in the sunrise
of the rejuvenating morning.
It looks like white clouds lurking around the solemn blue sky.
It sounds like the sounds of music being sung proudly
at the top of the highest hill.
But what's best is that it feels like whatever you want.

Thomas Dunn (13)
Lynn Grove VA High School

Wakey, Wakey

The house is in silence,
I'm fast asleep,
When all of a sudden,
I hear *beep, beep, beep.*

'Oh no, is it morning
Already,' I said,
For I am all snuggled
Up warm in my bed.

Now I hear noises,
And footsteps about,
Lights turning on,
The occasional shout.

Soon I smell bacon
And is that some toast?
All hot and all buttery -
That's how I like it the most.

Should I get up yet?
No, five minutes more.
Then all of a sudden,
Mum opens the door.

There's a jingle and a clink,
As she picks up the keys,
'Come on now, Sleepy,
Hurry up please.'

All right then,
Now it's time for my jog.
How I love mornings,
And being a dog!

Emma Redfern (12)
Lynn Grove VA High School

Hallowe'en

Children wake up,
They choose what to wear,
They choose where to go,
And who's in for a scare.

Will it be you
They're coming to scare?
Planning and scheming,
They could go anywhere.

The evening is here,
Children prowl the streets,
Looking to trick people,
And pick up some treats.

They come to your house,
A knock at the door,
Give the children sweets,
But they just want more.

The clock strikes twelve,
It's the end of the day,
As the children sleep,
Ghosts and ghouls come out to play.

So they call it trick or treat!

Liam Newson (12)
Lynn Grove VA High School

Death

Hold on tight,
Among the flight,
Run for your lives,
Because the guys have knives,
Envy no, hatred yes,
That's all they want,
Death, death, death!

Ian Smith (12)
Lynn Grove VA High School

Dark Times

Until October we all feel fine but at its end we change the time
The light of days give into dark, it ends the summer walks in the park
The signs of winter are now nigh
The cold, crisp nights now fill the sky
The warmth has left until next year
It's then we will again feel cheer.
We long to hear the new bird sing
When it goes we've again reached spring
Another winter has come to pass
Strong is the smell of new-cut grass
The darkened days give into light
Until next year goodbye dark nights.

Rebecca Bowles (12)
Lynn Grove VA High School

An Elephant

This is a poem about an elephant,
Who is tall and grey.
Every day he lays in the shade,
Just to pass the time away.

This is a poem about an elephant,
Who is large and round.
He has a long trunk,
That will swish you to the ground.

This is a poem about an elephant,
Who is small and sweet.
Even though he plays in the mud
His hair is always neat.

This is a poem about an elephant,
Who is big and bold.
When he gets hot he stands in the shade,
But then he gets cold.

Tanya Hodds (12)
Lynn Grove VA High School

Squirrel Nutkin And The Seasons

Squirrel Nutkin gathers nuts in autumn
His favourite time of year
Golden, crispy colourful leaves
Pleases him and his squirrel friends

Squirrel Nutkin sleeps in the winter
Plenty of food to go around
Warm and cosy in his home
How boring it does get?

Squirrel Nutkin plays in spring
Oh how he loves it so
Sunsets he enjoys watching
Beautiful and bright.

Squirrel Nutkin leaps in summer
Sunshine shining gleam
He washes himself in a birdbath
Delightful, lovely year.

Abbie Taylor (12)
Lynn Grove VA High School

Flying

I think flying is a blast,
Because at the start it is really fast,
It's like going up a giant hill,
Then it gets really still,
The plane food is really nice,
But I don't like some as it is rice,
We fly over a giant cloud,
But the noises are quite loud,
We float along really high,
I like being in the sky,
Up and down we sometimes go,
From here the clouds look like snow,
We are now touching down on the lane,
As I write this poem on the plane.

Liam Roberts (12)
Lynn Grove VA High School

School Holidays

My holiday started off great
I went to play badminton with my mate
But then the weather was rainy and bad
It got worse because jokes were being told by my dad
Saturday was good too
And teams on the football pitches were being booed
The week had ended
And after a hard week our telly was finally mended

One more week to go
And from Thursday to Monday the days have just flown
Town was the next adventure
I went and bought some games and it gave me great pleasure
I went round my nanny's for dinner
Then I went and played bowling at the bowl
My grandad went and played golf and put the ball in the hole

Back to school today
Not quite hooray
Lessons today were rather boring
Probably around this time my mum will be snoring
Homework for English as well
It turned out to be Hell
Ring the bell to go home please
So that I can take my dog to vets to get rid of his fleas.

Michael Rogers (13)
Lynn Grove VA High School

Saturn

S pinning through space
A mazing sight
T urning around
U nnerving storms
R ings floating
N ever-ending beauty.

Katherine Thurlow (13)
Lynn Grove VA High School

Chocolate

I love chocolate,
It goes down as a treat,
It swirls and melts,
And slips to my feet.

I'd eat it for breakfast,
Dinner and tea,
Not to be shared,
Every piece is for me.

Chocolate is creamy,
Comes in dark, brown and white,
It's yummy at day,
But delicious at night.

To eat some chocolate,
Is the best time of day,
I don't need to read,
And I don't need to play.

It's in my mouth,
All warm and silky,
The taste is so good,
So creamy and milky.

When it's all gone,
I feel so low,
I ate it so quickly,
Where did it all go?

It's down in my tummy,
Like a warm chocolate slush,
Mixing around,
But still tasting lush!

Gina Vettese (12)
Lynn Grove VA High School

My Poem About Poems

Poems have similes, metaphors and rhymes,
Some about romance, some about crimes,
Some about animals, cats and dogs,
Chameleons, caterpillars, bats and frogs.

Some have settings like somewhere hot and sunny,
Others at a circus with clowns that are so funny,
Some are in alleyways or someone else's house,
More are in pet shops buying a pet mouse.

Some are set in crowded places like a school,
Others in the town centre, the air is nice and cool,
Some are set in leisure centres or at the local park,
Some are set in daylight and others in the dark.

Some people in the poems are angry or sad,
Some are goody-two-shoes and others are quite bad,
Some are quite boring and others are fine,
But I like the ones with happy endings just like mine.

Hollie Grimble (12)
Lynn Grove VA High School

What We Dream Of?

P erfection, peace and prosperity,
A nger, done away with.
R ightness, riches and rightfulness,
A nger, done away with.
D istinction, dignity and delightfulness,
I llness, done away with.
S tateliness, success and simplicity,
E verything we dream of.

Francesca Watts (13)
Lynn Grove VA High School

War

War is grey with shadows of black.
It tastes like dust and clumps of mud.
It smells like a church with corpses on top
And looks like a dark room with light somewhere else.
It sounds like too much revenge is being dealt out.
War is harsh!

Daniel Savage (14)
Lynn Grove VA High School

Hallowe'en

Strange creatures all around,
Not one making a sound.
Flying and moving through the air,
It's Hallowe'en, so beware.
Bobbing apples and pumpkins lit through the night,
To give all a massive fright.
It's exciting with a chill in the air,
Hallowe'en, it's that time of year.

Scott Papworth (12)
Lynn Grove High School

My Horse (Haiku)

He canters so fast
His coat is like marmalade
He has eyes like gems.

Tyler Curtis (12)
Lynn Grove VA High School

Happiness

Happiness is the colour of bright yellow
It tastes like a sherbet lemon
It smells like a new day
It makes you smile
Puts a spring in your step
Sounds like your favourite song
Looks like a rainbow.

Jennifer Poole (12)
Lynn Grove VA High School

Birth

Birth is the brightest yellow
Birth tastes like the sweetest cake
Birth smells of the spring air
Birth looks like a field of newly born lambs
Birth sounds like cries of happiness
Birth is a new beginning.

Sophie Burgess (13)
Lynn Grove VA High School

Sadness

Sadness is the lightest blue
That tastes like bitter-sweet tears
Sadness smells like forgotten dreams
And looks like unwanted fears
Sadness sounds like empty words
And feels like nobody cares.

Lizzie Paine (13)
Lynn Grove VA High School

Sadness

Sadness is the colour of tears
It tastes like sea salt
Sadness smells like the pain of the suffering
Sadness looks lonely
And sounds like people calling for help
Sadness is never ending!

Jasmine Esherwood (13)
Lynn Grove VA High School

Once Hoped Forgotten

In a room so dark and grey
I wait all night, I wait all day
For someone who'll set my soul free
And keep it a distant memory.

I cannot help but feel the pain
Of the hurt that begins to gain
So will you please set my soul free
And keep it a distant memory?

Stephanie McKnight (14)
Lynn Grove VA High School

Bonfire Night (Haiku)

Rockets are flying
Fireworks are lit, bonfire burn
Colours exploding.

Matthew Thompson (12)
Lynn Grove VA High School

Dolphins

Dolphins are blue,
Dolphins are grey,
They are there for you and me every day,
But for how long we really don't know,
As they get killed by enemy and foe,
Sharp metal knives get stabbed through their skin,
And some of their body gets chucked in the bin,
Do you think this is any way to treat the lords of the sea
swimming under our feet?
No beast deserves this terrible fate,
Not even the worst, so why sit there and wait?
Get up and do something, don't let dolphins be bait,
Adopt a dolphin before it's too late.

Jessica Woodrow (12)
Lynn Grove VA High School

Bonfire Night

The sky is black and no sound is heard,
Then a distant sound like crackling occurred.
Bang!
Whoosh!
Wheee!
November 5th is here at last.
Warm woollen mittens and scarves are seen,
And the night is filled with colours that beam.
Children's laughter fills the air,
Stunning colours darting everywhere.
Toffee apples and sausages,
Everywhere you gaze,
All the air comes a bit of a haze.
But when you think it will never end,
The last firework is heard and the mood dampens again.

Charlotte Smith (12)
Lynn Grove VA High School

Alien's Point Of View

Fire in a box,
it's a torture room,
for dead beings.   *Oven*

Night and day,
awake or asleep,
at the touch of a button.   *Light switch*

Flood in a tube
controlled by wheels,
of unknown powers.   *Sink (tops)*

Hot or cold lakes,
hot when awake,
but cold when asleep.   *Kettle*

A cold mountain,
another torture place,
from fire to ice.   *Fridge/Freezer*

Cut pieces of beings,
spinning in water,
a dungeon of doom.   *Washing machine*

A sleeping object,
when poked,
it makes an angry noise.   *Stereo*

Thomas Gibbard (12)
Lynn Grove VA High School

Hate

Hate is an evil blood-red,
It tastes like coal-black toast,
It smells like a smoke filled room,
It looks like a haunted forest,
It sounds like the scraping of nails on a chalkboard,
It feels like standing in the cold with goosepimples all over.

Georgia Hanton (12)
Lynn Grove VA High School

Feelings

Love
Love is red
It tastes like strawberries and cream
It looks like a flower in the spring
It smells like freshly picked roses
It sounds like a romantic song
    Love makes us happy.

Revenge
Revenge is dark blue
It tastes like sour lemons
It looks like fire burning vigorously
It smells like burnt toast
It sounds like a barking dog
    Revenge makes us feel good.

Sharna Minister (12)
Lynn Grove VA High School

Love

Love is bright red
Love tastes like ripe, juicy strawberries
Love smells like new pink roses
It makes you feel happy and great
Love sounds like singing birds in the early, fresh morning
Love looks like a warm smile.

Courtney Dexter (12)
Lynn Grove VA High School

The Twister (Haiku)

Clouds getting wilder
Twister slamming down roaring
Speed getting faster.

Ashley Bond (12)
Lynn Grove VA High School

Throwaway

Down where the rubbish
is piled up high,
you will hear the sound
of laughing and cries.

Grubby and mouldy,
uncared for and forgotten,
children live
with rubbish that is rotten.

They're just like us,
they eat and sleep,
they don't have parents,
that's why they live so cheap.

There is just one problem
for the catchers they run,
but when they get caught,
it's not much fun.

Harm Kerkhof (12)
Lynn Grove VA High School

It's Winter

The sky is getting darker
The clouds are getting blacker
The air is much cooler
The ground is much wetter
It's winter.

All the time people are wearing coats
Most people have got their heating on
All it keeps doing is raining
People are constantly cold
It's winter.

Bradley Robinson (12)
Lynn Grove VA High School

The Little Dragon

I know a little dragon
Erin Thistle is his name
And sometimes when I'm walking home
I spy him in the lane.

Sometimes he can be quite bold
And others he's quite shy
I would love to play some games with him
But he won't although I try.

So I guess I'll have to be content
Just to watch him play
And hope that one day very soon
He will include me in his games.

Chris Gray (12)
Lynn Grove VA High School

TV Choice

So much to see so little time,
Channel to channel, what shall I watch?
What is the time?
Adverts and advertisements are such pain,
But in the end I cannot choose.
I watch a video I have already seen so many times before,
But in the end I got very bored
So I read the TV guide,
Films, soaps, documentaries or news,
Oh, I don't know what can I choose?
In the end I turn off the remote, run the bath and have a good soak,
I played with my boat and watched it float.
I watched more TV and went to bed.

Sian Keeler (13)
Lynn Grove VA High School

Bonfire Night

You know it's leading up to Bonfire Night,
Because people pay a penny for a guy to light.
There's fireworks in the shops and stores,
All different colours and shapes, so they're never a bore.

And as soon as you know it, it's here,
Bonfire Night, never a dull sound in your ear.
Sparklers alight and crackling away,
Bonfire's been lit, better keep the people at bay.

The guy is sizzling away on top,
While up above you can hear a bang and a pop.
The firework fountains screech and squeal,
All the colours definitely appeal.

The blues, greens, yellows and golds,
Purples, oranges and reds are all very bold.
The Catherine wheels turn and twizzle,
Wait until they stop and fizzle.

The fireworks go up in the air,
For all the people to sit and stare.
But most of all, my favourite bit,
Is when the guy is finally lit.

Alice Ramsden (12)
Lynn Grove VA High School

Sadness

Sadness is a horrible dark grey
It tastes like a bitter lemon
Feeling like sourness in your mouth
It smells damp and as cold as ice
Sadness looks like a deserted room
With nobody there to comfort you
It sounds of nothing but silence
Sadness is gloomy and dismal.

Alexander Stark (13)
Lynn Grove VA High School

Jamaica

J ammin' to the reggae rhythm
A ll of us together
M y family and friends
A ll sipping the Jamaican rum
I n the glorious weather
C ome and hear the sound of the steel drums
A s we jam in Jamaica!

Georgia Lewis (13)
Lynn Grove VA High School

Winter

Oh a lovely extra hour's sleep,
That should help for a new school week.

Summer's gone, winter's here,
Snow is coming, the kids all cheer.

The nights get darker one by one,
No playing out when school is done.

Wind and hail, rain and snow,
Are the delights winter has to show.

No more ice cream but steamed jam pud,
Boy oh boy that does sound good.

School is over hip, hip hooray,
Santa will be bringing his laden sleigh.

Back to school oh what a drag,
Shoulders ache from the weight of my bag.

An hour's sleep we soon will lose,
Making teachers blow a fuse.

Life seems so full of doom and gloom,
But not to worry spring's here soon.

Anthony Brown (12)
Lynn Grove VA High School

Autumn

The leaves fall off the tree
And float down to the ground.
They collect upon the grass,
Until the wind comes around.

The wind whistles through the tree
And lifts the leaves to dance.
It takes them in a moment,
The leaves don't have a chance.

The children come to play,
They kick leaves in the air.
They stuff leaves up their jumpers
And get them in their hair.

The autumn winds turn cooler,
Blue skies turn to grey.
The nights are drawing in now,
That winter's on its way.

Gemma Elliott (13)
Lynn Grove VA High School

The Wish Fish Dish

Sitting by the riverbank
Waiting for a fish,
Hoping to catch a big one
And serve it on a dish!

I'd really like to catch a fish
And have it for my tea,
But I'm sitting by the riverbank,
Now what can I see?

Yesterday I went a'fishing
Hoping for a fish,
Now I'm having my tea
And guess what's on my dish?

Lewis Chapman (12)
Lynn Grove VA High School

Santa's Stuck Up The Chimney!

Santa's stuck up the chimney,
Quick get him out with the tree.
'Ho, ho, ho,' he called,
'Thanks for helping me.'

I gave him some cookies,
I gave him some sweets,
I gave him some beer,
I gave the reindeer some treats.

He put some presents under the tree,
Most of them for me, me, me!

He waved goodbye and disappeared,
'Wait,' I said. 'You haven't drunk your beer.'
But it was too late; he had already gone,
I could still hear him whistling and singing a song.

So I went to bed
And snuggled up tight,
I cuddled my teddy
Until the morning light.

Lauren Halliwell (12)
Lynn Grove VA High School

Winter

W inter is my favourite season,
 I cy puddles on the ground.
N ights are cold and dark, with
T rees, rustling in the wind.
E arly morning mist and fog lies in the air, and
R ain and sleet falls from the sky.

Emily Crayston (13)
Lynn Grove VA High School

The Invisible Wind

Something is whistling through my hair,
But when I look nothing is there.

Something is pelting rain in my face,
But when I look there is not a trace.

Then I think to myself,
Who could do such a thing?
Moving things invisibly,
Quieter than a beat of a wing.

The wind.

It was the wind whistling through my hair
And when I look the wind is there.

It was the wind pelting rain in my face
And when I look the wind is there.

I realise how silly I have been,
To not have seen
That it was the wind.

Brett Robinson (12)
Lynn Grove VA High School

Winter Poem

In the winter when the snow is on the ground,
There are no animals to be found.
The snow lays soft and white,
Be careful you might get a Jack Frost bite.
Here strides Grandad with our presents,
In the other hand are four fat pheasants.
The snow has covered all the trees,
Then suddenly we feel a cold breeze.
The children are wearing hats and gloves,
Above their heads is a flock of doves.
Outside the snowman has a cold, round head,
Inside the children are wrapped up warm in bed.

Matthew Houston (12)
Lynn Grove VA High School

Hallowe'en (Haiku)

Spooky voices heard
The scary masks and costumes
Green ugly witches.

Liam Wooden (12)
Lynn Grove VA High School

In The Morning (Haiku)

In the morning breeze
Birds are singing with sweet sound,
Trees sway in the wind.

Casey Moughton (12)
Lynn Grove VA High School

Sparkles (Haiku)

Sun sparkles and shines,
Horses galloping wildly,
Grass is long and thin.

Lucy McNamara (12)
Lynn Grove VA High School

Sunny Beach (Haiku)

Sun on the light sand,
The yellow small grains are smooth,
You can hear the sea.

Aaron Hastings (12)
Lynn Grove VA High School

Tibby The Cat

I'm Tibby the cat
And despite what they think,
I'm the supreme huntress round here,
I savage the leaves,
I nibble at spiders
And dragonflies flutter with fear.

I'm Tibby the cat
And I'm my own boss,
I'll scratch where I like,
On the stairs or the chairs,
On the carpets and beds -
The scratch post's not for a tyke!

I'm Tibby the cat
And I'll lie where I like,
On clean duvets, shedding my fur
But my all time fave
Is the cardboard box,
Where I curl up safely and purr.

I'm Tibby the cat
And I'll do my own thing,
Only the best will do,
Hot barbecued food
And creamy milkshake,
Just remember I'm in charge - not you!

Andrew Greenwood (12)
Lynn Grove VA High School

Circus (Haiku)

In the circus ring,
Acrobats on the trapeze
Swaying side to side.

Amy Barnsley (12)
Lynn Grove VA High School

Roller Coaster

Here I am at the start,
Why am I here? I'm usually smart.
Going up, I'm so afraid,
Are you sure this ride has been made
Properly, because I can't see the rest,
Maybe I should stick to what I know best,
Just close my eyes and I'll be alright,
Close my eyes so very tight.
I see it now, I see the drop,
I feel like exploding, going pop!
Travelling now at break-neck speed,
Sitting at the front, I'm in the lead.
That's it, it's over - what a shame,
I want to go around again!

Jason Snowling (13)
Lynn Grove VA High School

Help (Haiku)

A piercing, shrieking,
Screaming wildly, 'Help me, please!'
'She is falling, help!'

Vicki-Louise Hurrell (13)
Lynn Grove VA High School

Armadillo

Armadillo scurries through the night,
Searching for insects to eat,
With its large front claws it digs with might,
Until it finds its morsel treat.
As the sun rises Armadillo moves back
And curls up in its burrow, to sleep.

Luke Rushbrook (13)
Lynn Grove VA High School

Victim

Have you ever thought,
About the people you have hurt
And everybody
That you have talked to
And how they think of you?
You've shattered all my dreams
With your shouting and your screams.
Drunken brawls and fights,
Ev'ry other night,
I start to see a theme.

Just leave me by myself,
I am, a person as well,
Not different to yourself.
I was yours.
So when you're dead and gone,
Hope you remember my face,
Feeling so withdrawn.
You missed out.

This message is for you,
That everything you may feel,
Taste, smell, see or hear,
Will die and rot away,
With you left to decay.
Nobody knows you more,
About how your life's been torn
By your stupid stunts
And how you confront
Your problems and your scorn.

Franki Buntain (14)
Lynn Grove VA High School

Ocean Sea (Haiku)

Ocean sea is calm
Waves battering against rocks
Sea is calm again.

Oliver Barnard (12)
Lynn Grove VA High School

Blow The Whistle

We watch the ball as they pass,
We hold our breath and wait
As the striker curls with class,
The goalie reaches just too late.

The crowd jump up with a roar
As the ball hits the net.
25 minutes gone, 1-0 the score,
The challenge has been set.

Second half the score's the same,
22 men still working hard.
We know it's only 'just a game'
And 'boo' at that yellow card.

Now the pressure is on,
The captain steps up,
Free kick, now it's 1-1,
Who will win that gold cup?

Extra time, it can't end in a draw,
Just 3 minutes to play,
With a header we add one more,
Not much left to say.

'Blow the whistle.'

Bradley Vlachos (13)
Lynn Grove VA High School

The Sun

The gleaming sun opening up like
A blossoming flower on a summer's day,
Beautifully shining through day to night,
Before being covered by the dark moonlit sky,
Then the sun reappears once again
And fills our sky with beauty.

Charlotte Groome (13)
Lynn Grove VA High School

Gleaming Trees (Haiku)

Gleaming trees blowing,
Swaying, moving in cold air,
Moving side to side.

Johnathon Bone (12)
Lynn Grove VA High School

The Fairy

She shivered with the cold
And huddled close to keep warm.
The rags she wore were no use,
Once elegant, now dusty and worn.

Her feet encased with mud,
Her hands were blue with cold.
Her wings were once colourful and bright,
Now are grey, tattered and heavy to hold.

She thought of happy memories,
Dancing and singing in the sun.
Her friends laughing by her side,
A smile on her face, having fun.

An ice-cold tear ran down her cheek,
Her skin was pale and full of scars.
A noise resounded, her eyes came alive,
Piercing blue, sparkling like stars.

Through the fog a shadow appeared,
Its steps pounding like a beating drum.
The shadow grew and the fog cleared,
Her body froze in fear, became numb.

A beautiful face stared at her,
Her former self mirrored there.
A soft, golden hand reached for hers,
'Come,' it whispered, eyes of love and care.

Jessica King (13)
Lynn Grove VA High School

A Guide To Tennis Strategies

There are many ways to play tennis,
To all of which you will need
A strategy to beat the best
And begin to always succeed.

What is the best strategy?
Do you always have to think
As a lot of players' strategies
Are just thought on court?

I can't give you the best one,
As I don't think I even know,
Because there's not a strategy
That applies to everyone.

So think up your own strategy
To win and to succeed,
And while you're thinking
Ponder this:

Is it always best to win?

Samuel Reynolds (14)
Lynn Grove VA High School

Why?

Why is there war and fighting?
It only ends up in tears,
Devastation left by destructive bombs,
People left in fear.

Why do innocent people die
In wars between two men?
Why can't there be peace and tranquillity
Instead of lives being stolen?

Why can't people get along?
Just forget about revenge.
Why is man so hateful?
Why? Why?

Laura Inal (13)
Lynn Grove VA High School

Titanic - The Unsinkable!

An unsinkable ship called Titanic,
All loaded and ready to go,
Passengers boarded, excited and waving,
What the future holds they don't know!

Sailing across the Atlantic,
Families enjoying their time on board,
They had no idea of the disaster
That was going to be in store.

On the night of 15th of April
The stars were shining bright,
But someone failed to notice
The iceberg looming in sight.

They thought the ship had missed it,
Oh what a lucky escape!
But no the Titanic was sinking,
Everyone realised this too late.

Panic to get to the lifeboats
But it soon became very clear,
Not everyone would be taken to safety,
So the passengers were shaking with fear.

Only a few were safe in the lifeboats
As the water started to rise,
The unsinkable was sinking,
Much to everyone's surprise!

On that fateful night in 1912
Thousands of people died,
If only there'd been more lifeboats
Many more people would've survived.

Remy Browning (14)
Lynn Grove VA High School

Autumn Days

Summer days have faded away,
The autumn days have come to stay.
Stepping outside and feeling the cold wind on my face,
Walking to my destination with a quick pace.
Leaves crunching beneath my feet,
All brown, scattered and far from neat.

Evenings are cold as the dark draws in,
Trees lose their leaves and their trunks go thin.
Raindrops hit the surface of my coat
And trickle down my sleeves in the shape of a moat.
The breeze blowing tiny raindrops at me from different ways,
Autumn days.

Bethany Fuller (13)
Lynn Grove VA High School

Journey Of A Cloud

I lay on the freshly cut grass,
Looking up at the sky.
My mind and thoughts wander
As I watch the clouds drift by.
Slowly but surely they travel
Beyond my sight.
They let the sun creep through them,
As it shines with all its might.
A long time after, most clouds
Have completely gone.
As they have a long journey
That they must carry on.
When their journey ends
Nobody knows.
But it'll certainly be
Wherever the wind blows.

Kayleigh O'Connor (13)
Lynn Grove VA High School

My Favourite Seasons

W inter is my favourite season,
 I t's the season when everything turns white,
N ever is there a warm day
T ill the spring comes back in March,
E very day I hope for snow,
R eady to make the best snowman yet!

S ummer is my favourite season,
U sually I go on holiday,
M any happy memories I have,
M aking new friends by the swimming pool,
E ven trying new foods that I hated,
R eally wanted to go back next year!

Emma Huggins (14)
Lynn Grove VA High School

Early Morning

The wind whistled and howled,
The trees danced from side to side,
A black cat scrambled along
A rickety old fence,
Whilst the gravel on the driveways
Were disturbed by the cars,
The whirr of the milkman's cart
Awoke the people of the street,
And the cheerful children were
Blown along on their way to school.

The frost and ice glimmered
On the windows of the cars,
The grass swayed in the wind
And the leaves of the trees
Blown to the ground by the
Unruly wind,
All these wonderful things
On a wonderful early morning.

Rachel Spry (12)
Lynn Grove VA High School

A Thought

Laying here makes me think
What we used to do,
You used to tickle me,
I used to tickle you.

Standing here makes me wonder
What our lives might be,
If I was up there for you
Or you were down here with me.

Sitting here makes me ponder
How we used to be,
Two peas in a pod,
That was you and me.

Sitting in my classroom
I think about our past,
When we used to play our games
And I always finished up last.

Often I think I see you,
Standing in front of me,
Then I remembered that,
You died when I was three.

Lisa Roberts (13)
Lynn Grove VA High School

Bonfire Night

Whooshing, slamming, fizzing, banging,
Blue, yellow and red
Shooting high into the sky,
Crashing around my head.

Crackle, fizz, crackle, hiss,
Zooming way up high,
All the noise and sparkling colours illuminate the sky.

William Randle (12)
Lynn Grove VA High School

A Touch Of Magic

The fairy kingdom was dark and powerful
And was hidden deep into the wood.
The fairies were mostly pleasant and kind
But some of them turned evil, if they could.

The evil ones no longer laughed nor cried
But slaughtered every living thing they passed.
They attacked their own family and friends
And their most dreadful spells were cast.

Many happy and loving fairies were killed
And the evil seemed like they would never be caught.
The forest was doomed and under threat
But then some good fairies had a thought.

They realised who the murderers were
And wanted them put away.
The fairies' wishes were magically granted
And in the end the murderers would pay.

The fairy kingdom regained its happiness
And fairies knew from then on there would be no more bad.
New fairies were born, old fairies died
And the wood remained cheerful, beautiful and not at all sad.

Zöe Knell (13)
Lynn Grove VA High School

Hate

Hate is black like the night sky,
Hate tastes like blood in your mouth,
Hate smells like a young boy's fear,
Hate is like looking down the barrel of a gun,
Hate sounds like a broken record,
Hate feels like you haven't got any friends
And you're all alone in your own little world.

James Lucas (12)
Lynn Grove VA High School

The Darkened Wood

The trees of the darkened wood
Shiver in the breeze,
You can hear the creaks,
The moans, the groans,
The chatter of the leaves.

The twigs of the darkened wood
Snap beneath my feet,
You can feel the crunch,
The creaks, the cracks,
The parts will never meet.

The grass of the darkened wood
Shimmer in the dawn,
You can see the moisture,
The dew, the hues,
The day it is reborn.

Victoria Clayton (13)
Lynn Grove VA High School

Hamsters

Noses twitching,
Beady eyes so bright,
Only wake up
In the middle of the night.

Always running
In their wheel,
Sniffing, searching
For their next meal.

Pouches filled,
Packed so tight,
Hamsters are at work
In the middle of the night.

Rachael Durrant (12)
Lynn Grove VA High School

A Nice Morning (Haiku)

Morning has come out,
Air is really calm and blue
While the clouds go past.

Kalie Rabbett (12)
Lynn Grove VA High School

Market Chips

Yummy, greasy market chips,
Unlike oranges that haven't got pips.

Some with vinegar dribbled on top,
Better than McCains from the shop.

Some flooded with gooey gravy,
The chips look like yellow ships from the navy.

Some with manky mustard,
That looks like gone-off custard.

Some with tomato sauce,
That squirts out with great force.

Some with curdled mayonnaise,
The taste sticks with you for many days.

Some with chilli sauce so hot,
It's debatable whether to have it or not!

Michael Riches (12)
Lynn Grove VA High School

Slippery Snakes (Haiku)

Hissing snakes slither
Slowly like an old tortoise
Waiting for their food.

Stefan Bylholt (12)
Lynn Grove VA High School

The Months Of Winter

In the months of winter
It gets cold and bitter,
So put on a coat, scarf and hat
And stay warm, do you know how to do that?
In the months of winter.

In the months of winter
You are freezing, start to jitter,
It falls with fluffy white snow,
Make a snowman do you know,
In the months of winter.

In the months of winter
The ice covers up the litter,
But now it's gone,
Let's get on,
No more months of winter.

Danielle Levitt (13)
Lynn Grove VA High School

My Half-Term Holiday

During this half-term I went on a trip,
I went to Portugal, some say it's quite hip.
Dad went and Jess, Nan and Grandad too,
The villa was nice, but the town was a tip.
When there I went swimming in our heated pool,
I kicked and I splashed, suppose I looked like a fool.
One day in a taxi we went up to town,
The journey was long so I started to frown.
The shops, they were great and I bought a load,
My nan she bought nothing, not even a gown.
We got home on Sunday at one in the morning
And when I woke up I could not stop yawning.

Reece Local (12)
Lynn Grove VA High School

Seaside Day

Today is a seaside day,
We can have fun, run and play.
Digging big holes in the sand,
Women on sunbeds trying to get tanned.

Small foamy waves crash onto the shore,
A bigger wave follows, then another, then more,
Destroying everything in its way,
Repeating this pattern day after day.

Rock pools form and the sea creatures lurk,
Crabs, shrimps and fish go about their day's work.
Dodging the nets, buckets and hands
Of the eager children all covered in sand.

The sun starts to set, the tide ebbs away,
The umbrellas go down, towels rolled away.
Dawdling up the steep, sandy way,
Tired children yawning, it's the end of the day.

Stephanie Ash (12)
Lynn Grove VA High School

Politics

What can I say about politicians?
They are just a bunch of loons
Filling up the television time,
When I could be watching cartoons.
When election time is over,
Let's all say, 'Hip hooray.'
No more boring news reports,
That cause me so much dismay.
Let's get back to normality,
Away from war and stuff.
So we can say at last,
'Politics,' we've had enough.

Daniel Chaplin (14)
Lynn Grove VA High School

What Am I?

They pour the prisoners into their doom,
They trap the light and freedom out with a lid.
They turn a switch and they scream with pain,
After some time they release them.

Answer: making popcorn.

Shaun Waters (12)
Lynn Grove VA High School

Revenge Is . . .

Revenge is a rich royal green,
It tastes like a sour lemon,
It smells sweet,
It looks like a hot burning fire,
It sounds like a distant scream,
It feels nice . . . after!

Tazmin Downing (12)
Lynn Grove VA High School

Peace

Peace is white,
It tastes like vanilla ice cream.
Peace smells fresh,
It looks like a dove,
It sounds like a bird singing gently,
It feels like spring when the blossom
Is falling off the trees.

Amy Newson (12)
Lynn Grove VA High School

An Alien Riddle

A monster with a huge mouth!
Teeth join together with a small tag,
It gets fed long lead sticks that produce sketchy marks
At the flick of a wrist,
The teeth snap together, only to be unclenched again in a short while.

Benjamin Forbes (12)
Lynn Grove VA High School

Comfort

Comfort is a nice faint orange,
Comfort is the smell of hot chocolate,
Comfort is the sound of classical music,
Comfort feels like a nice warm fire,
Comfort is home.

Daryl Hewett (12)
Lynn Grove VA High School

Shyness

Shyness is pale grey,
It tastes bland,
It smells damp but doesn't look like anything,
Just faded into the background.
It sounds like the silent tapping of water
Falling far into a sink.
It feels lonely and weak.

Alexandra Southgate (12)
Lynn Grove VA High School

Peace/Hate

Peace

Peace is a pure crystal white,
It tastes like freshly picked strawberries
And smells like the fresh air on a spring day.
Peace looks like a cheering crowd
And sounds like applause, with not a boo in the world.
Peace feels breezy and cool.

(But not all life is fresh and breezy,
Not all life is a cheering crowd,
Not all life is crystal white,
On the other hand, there is . . .)

Hate

Hate is scarlet, a dark blood-red,
Hate tastes like food in trenches.
It smells old, dark and dusty
And looks like bicarbonate of soda with vinegar.
Hate sounds like dying men in no-man's-land.
Hate feels like salt rubbed in a fresh wound.

George Mill (12)
Lynn Grove VA High School

Flying Creatures (Haiku)

Birds flapping their wings,
Swooping in the sharp, cold air,
Gliding through the wind.

Cathryn Clarke (12)
Lynn Grove VA High School

Pride And Happiness

Pride is blue, black and silver,
It tastes like tears on a happy day
And smells like bread freshly baked,
Looks bright and happy,
Sounds like a cheering crowd,
Feels like Chelsea winning that final
Match of the season.

Happiness is orange and yellow,
It tastes like nothing on Earth,
Smells like flowers freshly picked,
Sounds like a newborn baby,
Feels like laughing and crying put together.

Natasha Elby (13)
Lynn Grove VA High School

What Is Love?

Love is an orange and purple sunset
On a warm summer's night.

It tastes like melting chocolate
Oozing in your mouth.
It smells like freshly baked bread
Filling up your senses.

Love looks like big warm eyes
Staring up at you from a newborn puppy.

It sounds like the soft play of violins
While cruising down the River Seine.

Love feels like a kitten's silky fur.

Suzanne Garwood (13)
Lynn Grove VA High School

Revenge

Revenge is great,
There's nothing to hate,
It glows with a smug look on your face,
It tastes so sweet,
The redness has nothing to defeat.
Revenge is great,
With every rhythm and beat.

Lucy Evans (12)
Lynn Grove VA High School

Rage

Rage is black,
Rage is red,
Tastes like a lemon,
Smells like the dead,
Looks like the Great War in 1915.
Sounds like a bomb,
Let off by a terrorist team.
Rage feels rough,
Like a scuff on the knee.
It's painful to feel
And it's painful to see.

Tiffany Sarjeant (14)
Lynn Grove VA High School

A Rough Day At The Beach (Haiku)

Thundering sharp waves,
Stretching across the sand bed,
Crashing against rocks.

Sabrina Brothers (12)
Lynn Grove VA High School

The Ballad Of Titanic

Sunken in the Atlantic,
Dragged down by the deep blue pool,
Early in April '12,
The largest ship of all.

A forty-six thousand tonne boat on
A cold, calm, clear, chilled night,
Travelling at nearly top speed
There came a terrible sight.

Some lookouts saw an iceberg
And shouted down below.
People scurried round like ants
But still the ship did go.

She hit it with extreme force
And damaged the hull plates.
The first five rooms were flooded,
They shut all the doors and gates.

Slowly she was filling up,
The lifeboats all took sail,
Some people were jumping off
And others hung onto the rail.

The boat was broken in half
So many people drowned,
They were crying, dying,
Swimming round and round.

Over fifteen hundred deaths
And lifeboats full to the brim.
A lot of frozen bodies,
The future very dim.

The unsinkable ship of dreams
Was killed by a big mistake.
She's now become a legend
With love no other could take!

Mallory Spencer & Emma Bond (13)
Methwold High School

Irritating Sayings

In class the other day I felt such a twit,
When teacher turned and looked at me and yelled just, 'Sit!'

'Do your tie up!' she hissed in my ear,
'Or you'll sure get a detention of that I don't fear.'

'Where is your homework!' Teacher said with a smirk,
'And while you're looking for it tuck in your shirt.'

'Are you chewing gum?' the teacher did say,
'Cos if you are you will not go to play.'

'Do you want a detention?'
This is always mentioned.

'A chair has four legs, stop balancing on two,
Cos you're bound to fall off and we'll all laugh at you!'

Samantha Foster (12)
Methwold High School

D-Day

Into the boats, the soldiers went,
Into tanks, guns and trucks,
Weighed down, back bent,
Sitting, thinking of the battle.

Boats were bobbing up and down,
Men tossed from side to side.
Feeling sick, they start to frown,
Sitting, thinking of the battle.

They land; they exit on the beach,
Shooting at their enemies.
Many fall out of reach,
Dying, thinking of the battle.

The brave men fought for us all
At the D-Day landings.

Aaron Parkin (13)
Methwold High School

The Magic Box

(Based on 'Magic Box' by Kit Wright)

I will put in the box . . .

The stars that have shone for a thousand years,
The ocean so deep and so calm,
The clouds that can be any shape or size.

I will put in the box . . .

A moonlit dancer on a snowy peak,
A cold winter's night by the fire,
A cup of cocoa before I go to sleep.

I will put in the box . . .

The amazing feeling of love's first kiss,
The happy feeling of a friendly hug,
The feeling of acceptance with a friendly handshake.

I will put in the box . . .

Flames from the centre of the Earth so bright,
The sun's rays glistening on a beach
And the look in the eyes of the wildest lion.

My box is fashioned from the jewels of a dragon's cave.
The lid is the biggest shell of the ocean
And the inside is the silk of a silkworm.

I will ride from my box on Pegasus white
And land on cloud nine
And there I will lock and I will keep
My magic box in my mind so deep.

Roberta Sander (13)
Methwold High School

My Favourite Animals

It could be a monkey swinging from a branch,
Eating bananas in the middle of France,
Swinging from tree to tree,
Or maybe my favourite animals are bumblebees.

Buzzing around flower to flower,
Bumblebees are full of power,
But mess with a bumblebee
It's like playing with fire,
My next animal is round like a tyre.

You might have guessed it's a snake,
I would feed it chocolate cake,
It would slither gently across the ground,
It would be worth a hundred pound.

Or maybe a dolphin to jump out of water,
Of course it would have to live in Malta,
It would play around, no care in the world,
The problem is it could never be held.

The last animal is a dog that wouldn't howl
And people would smile and say, 'Wow.'
It would run like the wind
And run up to me and kiss my chin.

So that's the animals I would like to own,
But if I did my mum would moan.

Kelly Leat (12)
Methwold High School

Threpence! Threpence!

'Threpence! Threpence!'
An old man called,
Kind of strange,
Because he stood outside my door.
'What do you want?'
Came my reply.
He was kind of creepy,
Because he gave me the eye.
'Threpence! Threpence!'
He called out loud again.
Getting quite annoyed,
I told him there and then,
'If you don't let me be,
I'll ring the coppers!'
Just then something caught my eye,
A large crowd of shoppers,
To them I shouted, 'My oh my!'
'Threpence! Threpence!'
Came their reply.
Really annoying,
So I gave them the eye!
'Threpence yourself!'
I said, shutting my door,
Staring at the ceiling,
Staring at the floor.
'What on earth is happening?'
Said I to myself.
Then my heart was thumping,
Voices came from all around.
They screamed like they were dying,
A very frightening sound.
'Threpence! Threpence!'
Heard them punching at my door.
I screamed, 'You lousy loser!'

As I crashed down to the floor
Shattered glass upon me,
People came from all around,
I cried to them to let me be,
But they all stood their ground.
'Threpence! Threpence!'
Old, young and wise,
My whole house bombarded
With their never-ending cries!
'Threpence! Threpence!'
I yelled out loud again,
I ran into an open door,
Tripping up, there and then.
Suddenly, they were too quick,
They hit me hard
With a threpence stick.
Threpence is as threpence does,
As I ran and got hit
By a yellow threpence bus,
I yelled out loud, 'That really hurts!'
And to add to my great fortune
Came forth bootlegs and starts,
One final look up,
I was really surprised,
To be stared upon
By tearful eyes.
'Long live Threpence!'
Were my last words,
I hated those people,
Those maniacal nerds.

Michael Smith (14)
Methwold High School

Teachers

'Get to your next lesson,
Don't run in the hallway,
Line up outside in *silence*,
And do what I say.
Please come in,
I said be quiet and
Put that chewing gum in the bin.
Stand behind your chairs,
Take off your coat and
Get into pairs.
Now you can sit down,
Take out your planners
And copy the notes off the board.
Where are your manners?
Take that look off your face,
Do up your top button
And stop acting like a clown,
Just stop messing about,
Some people are here to learn,
That's it get out!'

Hollie Ball (12)
Methwold High School

Irritating Teachers

'Stand up, sit down,
Who do you think you are?
The class clown!
Five bars on your tie please
And tuck in your shirt,
It's down to your knees
And where is that homework I gave you to do?
I don't want excuses.
No, you can't go to the loo!
Get on with your work, concentrate,
I want silence please,
I shouldn't have to wait,
Will you sit up straight?
Stop passing notes to your mate.
Give me your planner,
Detention at lunchtime.'
The teachers make it look like such a crime.
Why is it that teachers make such a fuss?
But carry on teaching us!

Alexander Sellers (12)
Methwold High School

A Tribute To Ayrton Senna De Silva

It was very dark that day,
When a young driver's life was cut short,
'Racing is in my blood', he used to say,
Until that dreadful summer's day.

Ayrton Senna De Silva was his name,
Three times champion in the Williams,
Winning Formula 1 races brought him fame,
No one thought he'd ever race again.

1st May 1994 was very sad,
When the Brazilian crashed at Imola,
All the competitors were feeling bad
And no one anywhere was feeling glad.

He is still remembered to this day,
Because of his commitment to the sport,
Remind yourself, because I say,
'Remember Ayrton every day.'

Jamie Randall (13)
Methwold High School

Elvis Ballad

Elvis was a legend,
He came from Tennessee,
He was a god of rock 'n' roll,
A great dancer was he.

He made his own movies,
He married Priscilla Beaulieu,
They had a daughter Lisa Marie,
But life was to treat them cruelly.

As Elvis rocked the USA,
His records sold in their millions.
He rocked all day, he rocked all night,
So he must have made billions.

He died on June the 26th,
In 1977.
The whole world cried with sorrow,
His soul went up to Heaven.

Nathan Sismey (13)
Methwold High School

Night

Birds sleep, dusk falls,
Night creeps into her black world,
The smell of earth fills the air as night settles in.

Hedgehogs creep, crickets leap,
Badgers grunt, foxes hunt.
In the middle of the night,
So much life is around.

When day comes,
All that is left of the night
Are some golden brown feathers from the foxes' midnight meal.

Jessica Collinson (11)
Norwich High School for Girls

Destruction

The Earth shakes as the sky, filled with hatred, howls.
The tears from Heaven cascade an everlasting torrent.
The spears from Hell pierce the ever-blackening sky -
The only lights to be seen.
The crash of thunder as the Devil rides out and fills the ears of those
Rash enough to listen.
The darkness goes on forever, no escape from evil clutches.
It will not give in, nor will it let go, not before it has what it wants.

This uncontrollable force, so violent, brutally blots out any sound
Except that of its own.
The spears from Hell blaze brighter,
Brighter still is the fire that now highlights the sky.
The trees once tall and green now shrouded in flame,
Gasping for breath, enveloped in smoke.

The Earth shakes as the sky, filled with hatred mellows.
Tears from Heaven waver until none fall.
The spears from Hell stilled, no longer pierce the black sky
The Devil no longer rides out; he is still.
Has quickly given in, has let go, has what it wants,
As quickly as it came it went, leaving a trail of destruction in its wake.

Jade Seaman (13)
Norwich High School for Girls

The Thing

The black shadow covers the street,
Has fifty arms and fifty feet.
The body's the size of sixty men,
All night it's here, all day in its den.
Roaming the street in search of food,
Grinding on people, their pets it chewed.
The sight of sunlight the thing will flee,
Running to the coast and out to sea.
Making waves as it goes along,
The villagers are so glad it's gone.

Anna Wasden (11)
Norwich High School for Girls

Nightmares

Some can be scary
Some can be strange
But when you wake up you're looking around
Has the monster come out from your dream
Is it waiting behind the door
Or in a dark corner?

Then there is a bump and a crash
It's there: the monster's in your house
You're stuck, you can't move or shout for help
You can't shut your eyes in case it creeps up on you.

In the bed you lie there all night
And don't get any sleep
Then morning comes and you forget everything
But then night draws in
There's nothing you can do
It's time for bed and the
Nightmare begins again.

Lucy Cross (11)
Norwich High School for Girls

Night-Time

Bats swiftly fly over rooftops,
Barn owls settle in the corner of a shed,
Cats prowl silently through the grass in search of food,
The moon shines on the lawn, brightening up the night-time sky,
Stars twinkle making patterns of endless numbers,
The grass sways gently in the cool, midnight breeze,
The statues cast haunting shadows that look like ghosts,
Lamp posts lighten the way for drivers on their way home,
Nothing at night is easy to see except for a cat with bright yellow eyes,
Night-time can mean lots of different things,
Scary animals, nightmares or even dreams,
I find night-time interesting,
But I still think there might be something lurking, around corners.

Charlotte Ranson (11)
Norwich High School for Girls

Night Rider

I am riding through the forest
On my beautiful steed.
His mane is silver,
As silver as the moon
And his coat is black,
As black as the night.

Over hills and valleys
We ride in unison,
Together we are one.
Away we ride,
Away from anger, hate and fear,
Away from the world.

Darkness creeps over us,
Only visible are the moon and stars.
His mane lights up,
As if it were a torch
Shining through the sky,
Lighting the way.

Through the darkness we ride,
Our path is lit,
The way clear.
I feel his body tense
As he hears a sound,
But I know I'm safe.

And then we return
To our world
And the night sleeps,
As the birds sing
And everything is normal.

Georgina Drewery (11)
Norwich High School for Girls

One Blade Of Grass

Imagine
One blade of grass
Against
A great oak.

Imagine
One leaf
Against
Autumn's own rustic snow.

Imagine
A queen bee
Against
The king of the jungle.

Imagine
Us
Against
The Earth.

Imagine,
Imagine us.

We don't seem so big any more.

Alice Campbell Davis (12)
Norwich High School for Girls

After The Fireworks

The silence seeps through holes in the sky
And as we stand it hangs about us like cobwebs.
It's eerie and dark, the light is burnt out.
The fireworks have faded into the night
And in their wake comes this still silence,
Which chases away the joy that filled the air,
Not long before.

Helen Falkner (11)
Norwich High School for Girls

The Four Seasons

Autumn

When the leaves go red
And the fireworks explode
As Hallowe'en scare us.

Winter

When Christmas comes
As the wolf howls in the snow
And the ice melts.

Spring

When the flowers bud
And the fluffy chicks are born
As the sun rises.

Summer

When the ice cream appears
And the sea whirls around my feet
On the yellow sand.

Georgina Starling (11)
Norwich High School for Girls

Colours Of Heaven

Deep peachy-red of the early morning sky,
Graceful green of the great African forests,
Like nothing in the world,
The colours of Heaven.

Purples, blues, yellows and pinks of all the beautiful,
Flowers spread across the land,
The summer fruits ripe, juicy and ready to eat,
Like nothing in the world,
The colours of Heaven.

The secrets of Heaven will never be revealed,
The colours of Heaven,
Who knows?

Iffath Hossain (11)
Norwich High School for Girls

Christmas Memories

The Christmas tree stands there
Decorated in jewels,
With tinsel and reindeer
And bright coloured baubles.

A stocking is put
At the end of my bed,
To go from being empty,
To full of toys, instead.

She comes down the chimney,
His reindeer in a pack,
He goes to every house,
He needs a pat on the back.

I run down the stairs
To see the Christmas tree shining
And there under the beautiful tree
Are lots of presents, with colourful linings.

Christmas is a time for family cheer,
Don't let anything let you forget it.
If you don't give love on Christmas Day
You'll feel so sad, you'll regret it.

Beth James (11)
Norwich High School for Girls

Autumn

A gust of wind, a shower of leaves,
U nder a blanket I'm going to sneeze,
T ightly cuddle soft, brown ted,
U nder the covers asleep in bed,
M agical as autumn may be, winter is coming,
    autumn is going,
N ow warm by the fire with winter,
    along with it comes snow.

Rachel Mumford (11)
Norwich High School for Girls

The Week As It Goes

Normally I can't write for toffee,
But for you I'll give it a go.
So here you are, this is my poem
About the week as it goes.

When it comes down to Monday,
People are still half asleep.
They've still got hangovers from Saturday night,
Even though on Sunday they were asleep.

On Tuesday it gets even worse,
They're not just tired they're grumpy.
For many, the week has started to take its toll,
This means their hair has gone bumpy.

Thankfully on Wednesday things look up,
Everyone's happy and awake.
Last night they managed to wash their hair
And not go to bed so late.

On Thursday it's really not that bad,
People just start to get annoying.
They're all hyped up for the weekend ahead,
So for some this even means crying.

On Friday be sorry for the teachers,
They can't get a word in edgeways.
The kids just start to talk and talk,
No wonder the windows break.

At the weekend things liven up,
The kids go out at night.
They don't get back until 3am
So they're used to the morning light.

So there you have it, there you go,
That's the week of people I know.

Heidi Mobbs (11)
Norwich High School for Girls

Seasons

Baby lambs,
Ducklings too,
Flowers growing,
All is new.

Dewy grass,
A watery sun,
Colourful petals,
Spring has come.

Lush leaves,
Green turf,
Warm sea,
I need to surf.

Bright flowers,
Shining sun,
Juicy melons,
Summer is fun.

Fiery sun,
Blackberries,
Rosy apples,
Dark cherries.

Sunset leaves,
The skies are clear,
The air is cold,
Autumn is here.

Bare trees, frozen ponds,
Frost covers the turf,
Cold outside, warm within,
Snow covers all the earth.

Glittering whiteness all around,
Overwhelming the plants and earth,
The snow is cold but pillow-soft,
The world is waiting for the birth . . .
Of spring.

Flora Sitwell (12)
Norwich High School for Girls

Spring

Spring reminds me of fluffy golden chicks hatching in the warm nests
That their mothers have had to sit on for days and days.

It reminds me of the old oak tree suddenly coming to life,
Like a newborn baby
And the bright pink blossom bursting on a tree
Just outside my bedroom window.

It reminds me of the glowing, bright sun that looks down on everyone,
Watching every move they make.

Lastly, it reminds me of the newborn lambs that can't walk
And shake every time they stand up.
They look like a fluffy cloud going way, way up into the scary sky.

Spring is sparkly, spring is special,
Spring is definitely my favourite season.

Lucy Hardy (11)
Norwich High School for Girls

The Midnight Walk

The whispering wind made my hair swirl around my face,
I heard footsteps behind me so quickened my pace.
The moon above lit up the dusty track,
But the sky around it was pitch-black.
The rain poured down from the sky
And a nocturnal owl flew by.
I heard the footsteps again,
I began to run but then
The footsteps got faster and
Then on my shoulder I felt a hand.
I was near the end of the road,
So I ran across the grass freshly mowed.
Then I saw the light
And everything was alright.

Olivia Stevens (11)
Norwich High School for Girls

I Wish I Was . . .

I wish I was a little red fish
Swimming in the sea,
But a shark might come and eat me up,
That's not the life for me.

I wish I was a monkey
Swinging in the trees,
But I might get tired of doing that,
It's not the life for me.

I wish I was a lion
Prowling proud and free,
But it might be hot in Africa,
That's not the life for me.

Maybe I'll stay human
And wander in the breeze,
Animal life is lovely
But not the life for me!

Catherine Bates (11)
Norwich High School for Girls

Which Pet?

I think I'd like a lion,
So we could roar and prowl and fight,
But I think that all my family,
Might get quite a nasty fright!

I'd maybe have a kangaroo
And we would jump around all day,
But if we broke Mum's china,
I do not think he could stay!

Or what about a crocodile,
We'd surely have some fun,
But I'd have to be quite careful,
I might end up in his tum!

Elizabeth Hook (11)
Norwich High School for Girls

The Seagull

The wind blows
The fine sand
Down the moonlit shore
Towards the sea,
Shimmering blue.

The moonlight shines
As the fish dive
Into the deep blue depths.

Then the stillness is stirred,
A deep shriek above,
The fish disappear,
The wind is stilled,
The seagull has returned.

The seagull soars
To find its prey,
It glides down to
The sand below.

Its beady eyes
Look out to sea,
To find the
Small, stray creature.

It spots it far away,
Spreads its wings.
Shrieks and soars up high,
Then plummets down
To catch its prey.
Then back to the rock,
His home.

Rosie Vavasour (11)
Norwich High School for Girls

A Beautiful, Magical Autumn Day

The golden sun rose over the lush green hills,
Spiralling a stream of honey sunlight on a seaside town in Wales.
Doves sang their beautiful song,
They flew up and over the huge orange sun
Which filled the town with life and joy.
And copper beech leaves fell dry and crisp,
The azure sea glimmered, glistened and sparkled.
And a small, prickly hedgehog,
Stuck his wet, cold nose out of his tiny warm burrow,
And started to collect hard, frosty nuts and ruby-red berries,
For the winter when he hibernates with his family.

Gabrielle Brasier (11)
Norwich High School for Girls

The Winter Witch

When winter comes:
The winter witch's hibernation is over,
The rivers have frozen,
The trees are bare,
The crisp, white snow is on the ground,
The winter witch awakes.

When winter comes:
The winter witch's hibernation is over,
People get ready for Christmas,
Out come the fake fur coats,
Jack Frost visits in the night,
The winter witch awakes.

When winter comes:
The winter witch's hibernation is over,
She comes out of her summer bed,
She makes potions with gruesome ingredients,
She cackles as she rides on her broom,
The winter witch has awoken!

Sophie Chapman (12)
Norwich High School for Girls

If I Could

If I wasn't here,
I'd wish to sit in a big bubble
Away from all my troubles.

Or go to a swamp
Where I'll swim with a crocodile
And if he cries, I'll make him smile!

For a day, I'd like to be a pebble
In the middle of a stream
And be hit by the sun's beam.

But if I was doing that
I wouldn't be me
And that's the best I can be.

Olivia Ampofo (11)
Norwich High School for Girls

Seasons Haikus

In spring life begins
Cute lambs bleating everywhere -
Favourite season.

Summer soon arrives
Laughing, playing every day
But autumn is near.

The green leaves turn red
And they crunch under my feet
Hallowe'en passes.

Winter comes with snow
And Santa Claus is coming
But snow runs from spring.

Charlie Jacobs (11)
Norwich High School for Girls

Million Pounds

I bought a ticket,
A lottery ticket,
My numbers all ending in 9,
By Jove I won a million pounds!
And spent it all on a Jamaican cruise
And a Ferrari to park in the drive.
When I came back the money was gone,
And my Ferrari was scratched to bits!
'Those kids,' I yelled, 'they did it themselves
And I reported them straight to the police.
The police wrote it off, just another prank,
Just grin and bear it.'
And so I did
And for the rest of my life,
I lived with the scratched Ferrari on the edge of the town.
Never again did I buy a ticket.

Georgina Linton (12)
Norwich High School for Girls

How The World Was Made

The stars were made when baby spilt the glitter pot on the floor.
The sun was made when brother burnt the Christmas cake
and set the kitchen alight.
The moon was made when sister was naughty
and didn't eat her cheese.
The wind was made when big sister sneezed everywhere!
The rivers and rain were made when baby cried
for no reason at all.
The trees were made when big brother buried his broccoli
in the garden to rot.
People were made when sister dressed up dolls.
So that was how the world was made.
We children made the world.

Emily Wistow (11)
Norwich High School for Girls

Necessary

I'm normally OK at spelling,
But there's one word which gets stuck in my head.
Necessary.
'It is necessary to learn your spellings,' says Mum,
But I do not know how to spell it at all.

Is it necessary to flee from a big dog.
With baring teeth,
With flaring nostrils?
Is it necessary to stuff a big tree in his mouth
If he gets on my nerves
Or should I just flee for hours on end?

Necessary, is it hard to tell what is necessary and what isn't?
Is it necessary to go back and do normal school work,
Or can I stay here for the morning and just write?

Is it necessary to think about evil things,
When you watch a film about evil crows?
Is it necessary to think differently about crows from then on,
Or any type of bird even?

Is it necessary to think about dreams and nightmares,
Or should I just not bother
And leave them be.
Let them come and let them go.

Is it necessary to learn the word *necessary?*
It sounds the same when I read it out anyway,
So I'll just tell Mum I don't like spelling.

Lily Walker (11)
Norwich High School for Girls

Childhood

When you're a child,
Nothing *really* matters.
You're carefree, happy,
All day, play, play, play!

Spring
New things to explore, delicate flowers,
Newborn lambs and fluffy chicks.

Summer
Holidays in the sun, water slides,
Out all day messing around.

Autumn
Catching golden and red leaves,
And playing in the heaps of crackling leaves.

Winter
Pure crisp snow to play in, snowmen,
Snow angels and of course, *snowballs!*

But then, suddenly, you're an adult.
So much to do and so much to think about.
All day worry, work, worry,
Hardly a relaxing, carefree time.

What's the point of growing up!

Kate Dyer (11)
Norwich High School for Girls

The River

The river is a woven bed
of silk and pillows soft.
She cradles the ducks
the swans, the fish,
into her welcoming warmth.
The mallards click
the insects whirr
the heron standing silently
still, the river coughs up a
fish for him.
The heron darts,
salutes his thanks
and is gone on the wings
of the wind.
She winds her way
through the marshes
and woods.
The willows bow to
her harkening crown.
The mother of all peace.
The river flows on
she gets to a cliff
and her life is thrown away
into the sea.

Laura Butters (11)
Norwich High School for Girls

Friends

They can make you cry to sleep,
or with laughter.
They can make you weep,
they stand by you night and day,
from the first of June to the last of May.
They comfort you when you're feeling down
and they cheer you up as quick as a clown.
With them you can have a great laugh
and act as thought you're really daft.
Then you have fights that last all day,
by morning it's forgotten all out of the way.
For friends are for to forgive and forget
and there are still friends you haven't met,
for friends are great (most of the time)
And everyone should have some,
To keep forever.

Alexander Fuller (11)
Norwich High School for Girls

An Early Hunting

As the sun rose,
And the birds sang,
A cool breeze whistled through the trees,
Then a loud blast from a horn,
A pounding of hooves,
A small stampede of hounds.
They jumped the muddy ditch,
Then over the trickling stream.
Next horses thundered past,
Sweating, puffing, galloping,
Suddenly they all came to a halt.
The horses steamed and sweated.

Thoroughbreds, Irish draughts, cobs alike are tired.
They smelt of wildness itself,
Free and happy.

Hannah Talbot (12)
Norwich High School for Girls

The Garden Wall

I awoke early one morning
And sat at my window ledge
To find the garden glistening white
For it had snowed overnight.

I opened the window
And the sweet song of a robin
And the smell of fresh, crisp air
Filled my room.

I looked at the garden wall
And wondered why it was there.
For if it wasn't
The land would be everyone's.

I could walk and walk for hours
And never stop!
Not a care in the world.

Suddenly, the sound of a horn
And the yap of dogs
Filled my room,
For ugliness, war and the bare truth
Was on its way!

A red bushed fellow
Jumped,
Scratched,
At the wall
desperate to get over it,
For he knew that on the other side
He would be safe.
Safe in the beauty, peace and love.

By this time, the ugliness had caught up,
Let loose the mean eating machines.
They made a dash at the helpless fellow,
But this fellow was sly
And was not going to give up!

With one almighty leap,
He jumped into a bush,
And away through the fields beyond
He was free!

Away he flew,
Faster than a greyhound.
Ugliness controlled their beasts
And away they went,
To find the next, not so sly fellow.

Now I know why there is a garden wall
And how glad I am,
For it separates beauty, peace and love
From ugliness, war and the bare truth.

Sophie Kightley (13)
Norwich High School for Girls

Skiing

The gentle sound
All around
Of gently whipped up spray,

Hitting poles
Big loud thuds
The silence is disturbed,

Through the gates
Around the poles
Quickly as you flow,

Down the slope
Slipping, skidding
Almost falling over,

Through the gates
Around the poles
It's finished, it's all over.

Milli Rhead (12)
Norwich High School for Girls

Seasons

Springs comes as new year starts
Bringing new resolutions for me and you
Lambs and chicks newly born
And the sun shines in a sky so blue

Buckets and spades, coloured balls
Silver sands, hazy sun
Children running to ice cream stalls
Jumping, splashing, having fun.

Red, yellow, brown and gold
Falling all around
Silently they fall
Not making a sound

Everywhere is sparkling
Like jewels in a crown
The ground is all white
Like a beautiful ballgown.

Laura Palmer (12)
Norwich High School for Girls

If

If I could fly,
So high in the sky,
Among the cotton-like clouds,

If I could run,
Like a cheetah,
The hot sun beating on my back,

If I could swim,
Like a mermaid,
Not needing to breathe,
I would be free.

If only, if only . . .
It wasn't raining and
I was outside.

Hannah Robison (12)
Norwich High School for Girls

The Mermaid

Who would be
A mermaid fair,
Singing alone,
Combing her hair,
Under the sea,
In a golden curl,
With a comb of pearl,
On a throne?

I would be a mermaid fair;
I would sing to myself the whole of the day.
With a comb of pearl I would comb my hair
And still as I combed I would sing and say,
'Who is it loves me? Who loves not me?'
I would comb my hair till my ringlets would fall,
Low down, low down
And I should look like a fountain of gold
Springing alone
With a shrill inner sound,
Over the throne
In the midst of the hall.

Laura Thompson (12)
Norwich High School for Girls

Hedgerows

H edgehogs snuffle around on the ground
E ager birds enjoy the berries
D arting between the spiky brambles
G olden leaves appear from the green
E nding summertime!
R obins perch on the highest branches
O versized blackberries, ready for picking
W ind rustles the autumn leaves
S quirrels gather their winter supply.

Emily Applegate (12)
Norwich High School for Girls

The Box

I have a very special box,
Only one of its kind,
It came from my great auntie's house,
It was a great find.

One day she went on holiday
And never did return,
She stayed to live in Swaziland,
She liked the heat and sunburn.

She wrote a long, long letter,
To say, 'It is too bad,
But I'm happy here in Swaziland,
I bet you think I'm mad.

So I'm leaving all my treasures,
My house, my cat, my socks,
My wellies and my woollies
And of course my special box.

If you lift the lid
And have a look inside,
It may seem rather empty
And very long and wide.

This box held happy memories,
Which I'd like you to follow,
By adding all your treasures,
Through the years from tomorrow,

So add all the things,
That mean the most to you,
Like letters, cards and poems,
Photographs and trinkets too.

When you get to eighty
And run away like me,
To end your life with sunshine,
Then give the box to . . .'

Emma Cooper (13)
Norwich High School for Girls

The Weekly Shop

I don't like the weekly shop,
You walk around until you drop.
Shelves up high and shelves down low,
Round and round the shop we go.

The trolley it will not shift,
Much more of this, we'll need a lift!
Oh the shelves are so inviting,
All that food looks so enticing.

The things I want I cannot have,
Because Mum says they're all too bad.
So what is wrong with crisps and sweets?
A fat-free yoghurt's hardly a treat!

Now at last it's time to go,
There's one thing left to do and so,
A sticky bun without a doubt,
My special treat for helping out!

All right I'll do the weekly shop,
I'll walk around until I drop!

Alex Beatty (12)
Norwich High School for Girls

My Brother

When my brother is awake,
Lots of mischief he does make,
Making noises and throwing toys,
Just like other little boys,
A typical three-year-old he might be,
Knocking over coffee and tea,
Although I love him, sometimes he makes me weep,
But he's really sweet when he's asleep!

Hannah Greeves (12)
Norwich High School for Girls

Wonder?

I wonder, I wonder
Will there be peace all over the world one day?
Will people ever be able to say their thoughts
Without being judged?

I wonder, I wonder
Will people ever be able to travel at the speed of light?
Will prime ministers and presidents ever be able to
Compromise without starting a fight?

I wonder, I wonder
Will poor countries ever have a water pump in every town?
Will the sight of a butterfly be able to turn a frown upside down?

I wonder, I wonder . . .

Victoria Helman (12)
Norwich High School for Girls

Dreams

Dreams are seldom rare to come
They whisper through the air
When you go to bed at night
A dream awaits you there.

So silent, swift and gently come
To ease a weary mind
They caress troubles soft away
Strong and yet so kind

Some dreams are not quite what you thought
They taunt you in the night
Their malice rings inside your ears
Until the morning light

People all around the world
Are not quite what they seem
Those who are better off
Are those who quickly dream.

Hannah Malcolm (12)
Norwich High School for Girls

Highly Intelligent Life Forms

You may think you're clever
But really you aren't.
You may think you'll predict the weather,
But in actual fact you can't.

We can talk, we can walk,
We can even drink whisky.
We use a knife, we use a fork,
But are we really that frisky?

We can copy a picture,
But not really more than twice.
We're made of a strange mixture
And some people are inhabited by lice!

Do words go in one ear and come out the other?
Are you as thick as the walls of your house?
Can *you* answer a question or do you ask your brother?
The animal that's more clever than you is actually
A mouse!

Ani Mukhopadhyay (12)
Norwich High School for Girls

The Hooded Executioner

Convicted of rape, theft and murder,
Sentenced to death by shooting,
Tied to a stake and blindfolded,
His last words were, 'I'm innocent!
This is all made up!'
'You are convicted of over ten crimes!'
Cried the commander. 'Including rebellion.
Rebellion against this, the only free society!'
'This is not free,' cried the man.
Then the guns opened fire.

Guy Jackson (12)
Reepham High School

What Is Love?

L ove is like an animal twisting and tearing people apart,
O bedient and disobedient making people cry,
V oices in your head make you think about love,
E njoyable partnerships make you joyous with each other,

I gnorant people make you think,
S unny days are happy days,

A bout time you got a grip,
N asty things do come true,

A pple pie is sweet like love,
N ew babies arriving,
I love you,
M any things are done in a day,
A fter things are said,
L ove is spread, sugary contents eat your heart away.

Jade Cooper (12)
Reepham High School

The Meaning

Broken like a heart
What's out? What's in?
Prick your dreams on a pin
They flash like lights
Fly, fly to a distant shore
Flame to a flame
The ball rolling like a bowling ball
Baby claws that destroy nothing
Not even the soul that is the meaning of life
That poses no threat
Special to people of the world
Fire clock the life of eternity
Where nothing's what it seems
Burn you, burn you
The soul is the only meaning of life.

Randle Brooks (12)
Reepham High School

Cup Final

My nerves are jumping,
Legs like jelly,
The manager gives the sign.
We walked out of the dressing room,
Lined up in the tunnel,
Everyone with butterflies in their stomachs.
We followed the referee out,
A packed stadium
Fans chanting my name,
The national anthem rings in our ears,
Kick-off.
89 minutes pass, 0-0,
Our striker gets near the goal,
He is brought down,
Penalty!
The crowd roars.
I step up to take it,
I jogged to the ball,
I kicked it,
Bang!
We are the champions!

Barney Horner & Jamie Grimson (12)
Reepham High School

The Rose

Fold on fold the purest white,
lovely pink
and red so bright
buds to open and expose
perfect both to see and hold
loveliest flower that always
grows.

Charlotte Webster (11)
Reepham High School

Elephants Of Africa

Elephants roaming, big and strong,
With no care in the world,
Calling to their elephant friends.
The long grass of Africa under their feet,
Sometimes raining, sometimes sunny,
The elephants are there.
White tusks they use to fight and play.
Covering miles a day.
How much fun it would be to be an elephant,
An elephant of Africa.

Wandering to the water holes,
With their families,
Are elephants big and small.
Herding off the human poachers,
Sometimes men, sometimes women,
Feeding off the African plants.
How much fun it would be to be an elephant,
An elephant of Africa.

Rebecca Dawson-Tuck (13)
Reepham High School

Rock

My body is a rock
My skin is wrinkled leather
My head is kept cool by two giant fans
My eyes are wizened by the sights of years gone by,
I never forget
My legs are solid oaks
My tail hides as though embarrassed at its size
I live on the sunburnt plains of Africa.

Lily Tozer (11)
Reepham High School

Big Drop

He started with a 100 metre drop in
On the way down he seemed to go white,
His skateboard wheels went bright
And the sound of a scraped blackboard screeched.

Then the wheels came loose and flew,
He was just on the trucks, sliding down,
The wheels landed burnt and brown,
And he carried on sliding.

When he hit the bottom he jumped,
He and his deck flew across the air.
When he landed, everyone had a stare,
Then he got to his feet gently and went off
To *drop again.*

Oliver Barker (12)
Reepham High School

Waiting

When I got home, you weren't there,
Where were you?
I put my key in the latch,
The click echoed around the empty flat.
Where were you?
I stepped inside and called your name,
There was no reply.
Where were you?
I cooked you a meal,
I sat and waited.
Where were you?
You never came home.
Where are you?

Hattie Bowden (12)
Reepham High School

Autumn Is all Around Us

The autumn's coming,
The autumn's here,
The autumn's gone,
Autumn's gone,
Autumn's gone.

Pepsi snuggle up,
Hides, hides under the table,
Goes everywhere,
Ironing board, sink, washing machine,
Is everywhere,
Everywhere,
Everywhere.

Excitement grows,
Tree up, new place to go,
Tree and Christmas, great,
So don't let it go,
Let it go,
Let it go.

Cute, cuddly,
So sweet,
I love him,
He loves me,
We love each other,
Love each other,
Love each other.

Storm, all wet and scary,
We hide away.
This is the end,
Come the end,
The end.

Elisabeth Cook (11)
Reepham High School

Inliner's Spirits

He fell,
He fell on skates,
From a 20-foot drop.
His body,
What body?
Crashed, blood, shouting, screaming,
will he live or die?
No giving up with this brave person,
Goes again to land what he'd tried.
Oh my God, he's done it,
He's landed what he tried,
What a life to live,
Clapping, shouting, hugging, screaming,
Covers of magazines drenched with all the pictures.
What a life to live,
Autographs, handshakes. all day long.
Competitions, street and vert,
What a life to live.

David Vaughan (12)
Reepham High School

Whale

My body is a steaming train,
My skin is the blue sky,
My head is surrounded by water vapour,
My eyes are the lovely green grass,
My tail is swimming in the blue sea.
I live in the deep part of the ocean,
Where the fish are.

Gabrielle Tillson (11)
Reepham High School

Movies In Motion

She used to say,
Heaven knows Mr Allison
And they would have
An Affair to Remember.
They had a
Marriage on the Rocks.
It could be seen that he had found his
Dream wife,
They went on
The Journey
To
King Solomon's Mines
And went sky high with
The Gypsy Moths,
While their love lasted
From Here to Eternity.
A few years later they had a daughter, whom they called
Young Bess.
While they sat at their
Separate Tables
They had
Tea and Sympathy
For everyone.
A good thing they did not come across
The King and I.
And they would say
Quo Vadis?
To whom they met.
It was also a good thing that she is not
A Woman of Substance
And they would
Hold the Dream
While they walked in
The Chalk Garden
On a romantic night called
The Night of the Iguana.

Over the wall
The grass is Greener
And he would sit and read the paper about
The Prisoner of Zenda.
Each morning when she woke, she would say,
I See a Dark Stranger.
To make her feel better he picked a flower called
Black Narcissus,
After their son-in-law lost all the money at the
Casino Royale.

A month later, the man of the house
Listened to the story which was named
The Life and Death of Colonel Blimp.
The Day Will Dawn
And once again it would be
Love on the Dole,
And so it came
To
The End of the Affair.

Katie Robertson (13)
Reepham High School

Sun And Moon

The sun will come up, we will awake.
It will rise at half-past seven
And sink down at quarter to eight.
It will shine bright,
Bring us light.
Then the moon will take its place
And it will become night.
It glows at us, but brings us no daylight.

Amy Wiliamson & Sarah Clitheroe (11)
Reepham High School

Unrequited Love

I love him, but he doesn't love me,
I wish we could be together and live happily.
I've been pushed aside for years and years,
And I've shed one thousand tears.
My face is pale with bags under my eyes,
His girlfriend I really do despise.
'I try to be noticed, I really do,
But you don't return the love that I give to you.'

Kayleigh Wright & Bethany Skitmore (12)
Reepham High School

Tony Ogogo

A man came from far away Africa,
Came to The Clare School today,
To give us a workshop
Of music and play.
We really enjoyed his style,
He was cool and hip.
with stories and dance,
He took us on a long trip.
I liked the 'Tortoise' one best,
Tony had a pillow stuffed up his shirt.
The music had louds and softs,
Mr Smith had to wear an African skirt.

Ashley Sison (13)
The Clare Special School

Books

A library is a place
you can sit and read,
where the books
take you away to other places,
other times,
even meeting other people,
and yet you are still sitting there
in a library,
in an armchair.

Books are keys,
doors to other worlds,
you can be anybody you like
when reading or writing books -
but still you are sitting in your room,
or in the library.

I often find when reading
that I don't know what will happen next,
and when that happens
I am left to wonder
what is best for the characters
'What should they do next?'
Totally mesmerised,
I read on,
sitting in the library.

Iain McAllister
The Clare Special School

Salt And Vinegar Crisps

I like salt and vinegar crisps,
They make my lips wiggle if I eat too many.
If I drink too much 7-Up, my lips pop,
But salt and vinegar crisps are my favourite.
I feel so hungry, I could eat an elephant.
I wish it was lunchtime now
So I could eat my lunch now.
I eat like an animal and I scream like an elephant.
But best of all, I like salt and vinegar.

Nathan Griggs (13)
The Clare Special School

Sport

I love sport.
I like football.
I really enjoy scoring a goal best
When playing football.

I don't like basketball,
It's not my game.
The draw-card of sport for me
Is the winning!
Yippee, yippee!

Harry Hawes (13)
The Clare Special School

My School

My school is fantastic,
I like it a lot.
I get enjoyment out of being here.

I like assembly,
Mr Smith tells us loads.
I like my teachers
And I like break times and lunchtimes
And being with my friends.

I like the book fairs we have -
Books are great!
My school is fantastic,
I like it a lot.

Joshua Lobo (16)
The Clare Special School

Ode To Mrs Wiggins

Mrs Wiggins
Is the kind English teacher.
Lessons are great,
Learning on the take.

Things she does
Really reach ya.
She's so lovely,
Just like chocolate cake!

Thomas Docwra (13)
The Clare Special School

The Snowy Day

I get excited when I see snowflakes.
My friends and I play snowball fights.
We make snowmen.

I feel the snow carefully, it's soft.
The scenery is beautiful,
Like a snowy-white blanket.
I love the snow, it makes me happy.

Snow is fantastic,
But when it melts I am upset.
Maybe I will see it again next year?

Gary Cowell (15)
The Clare Special School

Teddy Bear

T iny
E veryone's friend
D early loved
D on't leave him behind
Y ou may not find him

B eautiful and full of fun
E veryone has to have one
A nd if you haven't
R un and get one!

Felicity Stafford-Allan (15)
The Clare Special School

I Love Cricket

I love cricket,
Cricket is fun.
When I go to cricket,
I watch the bowler run.

We like to take our picnic
And eat up all the buns.
We sit and watch the cricketers
Make a lot of home runs.

Jesca Hindley & Daisy Murwira (13)
The Clare Special School

Argue

Kids nowadays grow up too fast,
My fatherly advice is to make your childhood last.
Don't waste your time watching TV,
When you could be running wild and free.
When I was young, I never had the things you have today,
I used to go outside, all the time, to play.

> Why won't you just leave me alone?
> All you do is moan and groan.
> We aren't still in the 'good old days',
> You are just too stuck in your ways.
> What's the point in your complaining?
> Now we just don't need the caning.

For God's sake, money doesn't grow on trees,
You ask for this and that and never say please.
You treat this house like a hotel,
Living with you is like living in Hell.
Stop demanding and give me a break.
My throat bloomin' hurts and I've got a headache.

Matthew Rudling (15)
Wymondham High School

Our Lives

My life is here with whitewashed walls,
Where children laugh and play,
I do not know why I am here,
I understand not what they say.

My life is here in the vast expanse,
My skin, the ground is cracked.
The rain season come,
My home is gone once more.

My life is here on the basketball court,
Where all my life's a game,
Chicago Bulls power through,
I worry about little else.

My life is here in downtown Bronx,
It's not a life, a constant work place,
Where we all know the secret code
That keeps us from that place.

My life is here in the snow,
It's always here, nothing exciting,
A pain that keeps us in our homes
And keeps the supplies low.

My life is here with other girls,
Without a father, mother, home life,
A mission to complete exams,
With the grades they want to see.

My life is here in the British Isles,
Where the weather we can predict,
The co-ed schools run wild,
And different races mix.

Our lives are here on this world stage,
Where our lives are knit and *cut*.

Rachel Nichols (14)
Wymondham High School

How They Live

Small brown hands tap
on the window,
bracelets on their arms jingle,
faces look in,   hopeful
at the four inside.

Outside, bare feet shuffle
on the dry grass
and I see how they live.
My heart sinks
my eyes glaze over.

Banned from their wood shelter
till dinner.
They beg
            for anything
under the rays of the hot sun.

Pressed noses against the window
they still look in   hopeful
the car starts to move.
Crushed spirits
look on, down the road.

I look back wondering,
                is this how they live?

Hanna Puggaard Witt (14)
Wymondham High School

A Moment In Time

Waiting in the classroom,

Ready for the bell,

A blonde girl covered in grease sits,
Looking over at a stylish, well-groomed young woman,
Who sits casually filing her nails.

The chairs are next to each other,

Yet they seem so far apart.
She looked up at her idol as she brushed her luxurious long locks,
But the magnificent lady never noticed her.

The bell rings,
It was as if they never met.

Emily Spinks (14)
Wymondham High School

My Immortal

If I were a vampire,
I would love to fly,
Higher and higher
Up in the sky,

Watching,
Waiting,
For a lover
so I can kiss and kill.

If I were a mortal
I could walk on the ground,
I would use doors, not portals,
Earth would make a different sound,

Watching,
Waiting
For a lover
To kiss and love.

Megan Long (14)
Wymondham High School

Oak

Under the large oak he lay,
A boy, lost in his thoughts of days,
When they were there to comfort him,
He was happy then, but now he has to swim,
To save himself from them,
Not people, dreams, horrors of things that,
In their way, will scare you till you go astray,
And wish that you were never born,
And when you were, why you weren't warned,
That life was such a fragile thing,
One slip and you may have to cling,
To it, sit in a bed for years,
With nothing but eternal fears,
Of what might happen, when you sleep,
That life might leave you; creep away, inch by inch.
The boy, now a man, 23,
No money, life or anything,
A man walks past, drops 10p,
Not bothered by the pain, and suffering
Of the man, once a boy, so cold and thin,
The 10p man had pain to bear,
He lost his son so young, despair.
When he found his bag, the family broke,
Underneath the large great oak.

Josh Smith (14)
Wymondham High School

Empty But Full

Standing in the garden holding out my arm
I feel so empty, but yet guilty inside
I have lost such a *huge* part of me
Would he return I was yet to learn

I miss him now and then
But why should I care if he doesn't?
He had a choice but being every man he took the bad choice
I can't help but wonder why he left when I was younger

I love him dearly, but really I don't
They say blood is *thicker* than water
But is it really?
I love my stepdad more now than I ever had

If my true dad stayed would I still love him?
The situation might be different but because he left
Does he love me?
Love is through trust and not first lust of a feeling

He still sends me gifts
But the sight of him would please me more
In fact it wouldn't because of the anger that runs through my head
I wish he could see what he has done to me

Does he love his new family more than his old?
I know I do
I don't even see him, does that prove that
He can't bear the sight of me?
All my pain seems to drain away when I release myself

Although it still does not seem to help.

Emma Williams (14)
Wymondham High School

Home And Away

The city compared
To my quiet, small village,
Is a whole different place,
From an entire new world.

Serene, quiet, wide open spaces,
Full of bright, colourful flowers and trees,
Cute fluffy animals,
Rabbits, squirrels and little brown mice.

Smog and smoke clog up my lungs,
With dust and dirt.
Surrounded by deafening transport
Puffing out black, foggy fumes.

My comforting home,
Settled calmly in a tight, small community,
Friendly faces everywhere,
Stop to say, 'Hello.'

Many people,
Dull, plain, rich or poor,
Turn from every shady corner,
Round each towering skyscraper.

This strange world,
Changes from quiet to loud,
colourful to dull,
Why does it have such different lives?

Hannah Adcock (14)
Wymondham High School

Equality Is A Dream

The rich sit around their fireplace on their Italian silk armchairs,
crystal glass of brandy in their selfish, spotless hands.
> *The poor sit on the floor in a dark and gloomy room,*
> *The only source of light and heat*
> *are the candles dimming down.*

The rich walk away to eat their feast on their long mahogany table,
Mouth-watering roast beef, roast pork and 40-year-old white wine.
> *The poor realise that they'll have no food*
> *for the second day in a row,*
> *They go to sleep with fear for tomorrow*
> *as the torture restarts in the morning.*

The rich go to sleep in their four-poster beds,
Not a worry for tomorrow as it's a peaceful, calm day.
> *When the poor get up, they find their son dead.*

When the rich get up, they have marmalade on bread.

Alastair White (14)
Wymondham High School

My Angel

The journey has ended,
It had never begun,
My child never saw
The bright, burning sun.

Her very first breath
Was also her last,
Her life was stolen,
Her being is past.

Her shining blue eyes
Whispered goodbye,
I clutched her to me
And allowed her to die.

Lucy Spinks (14)
Wymondham High School

The Memory

The sun shone through the curtains,
the waves crawled up the stony beach,
the jolly sound of an ice cream van was in the distance.
He smiled.
The dust danced and played in the sunlight,
he stared at the brightly painted walls
and the wave pattern around the skirting board.
Laughing, he could hear laughter coming from the small children.
The clatter of the small, round and smooth pebbles on the shore.
The joy.
The peace.
The overwhelming feeling of calm.

The sun went behind the iron bar,
the rusting springs on the bed creaked,
the dull moan of a police car was in the distance.
He wept.
The dust had left the empty shell, he stared
at the concrete walls and the damp rising around the bottom.
Shouting, he could hear shouting coming
coming from a fight downstairs.
The clatter of the metal, round and hard dinner trays
being thrown around the hall.
The hatred.
The sadness.
The overwhelming feeling of remorse.

Ben Shackleton (14)
Wymondham High School

Popular

I wish I was one of the popular kids
Who'd have lots of mates
Everyone wants to be your friend
Always the centre of attention

I just sit in a corner
Nobody talks to me
Nobody looks at me
They don't even notice me
I'm invisible to them

I always hate sports
When we're picking teams at school
The captains pick all their friends
They argue over the best people
but
    one
       by
          one
Everyone goes, apart from me
I'm the last person left
No one wants me on their team
The captains argue over who gets stuck with me -
The loser
The freak

The bell rings - the end of school
Finally I can escape
The popular children all run off to the park
To have fun and laugh and do what normal friends do
I go home
Another day gone

I wish I was one of the popular kids.

Olivia Jones (14)
Wymondham High School

Some Days

Some days my eyes
burn in their sockets,
No matter how hard I try to stop,
The heaviness of the water always wins,
Streams of it
trickle
down.
I can taste the salt on my lips.
My lungs feel like they have been shredded,
Each breath burns my chest. I quiver;
I try to calm down,
But I'm not in control.
I wait for the storms to end . . . waiting
Shaking, irregular breathing so painful,
My face, all red and moist.
Finally I'm in control again, I wipe my eyes
Take a deep breath and carry on living in this world . . .

The days when my mouth cannot help but to smile
My body feels full of life and anything is possible.
Nothing can stand in my way today,
Not even negative thoughts, not even emotions.
The world seems a colourful place today.
The grey clouds have shifted and the sun shines
and has dried up all my tears. Today I'm happy.
I feel happy to be alive, I feel grateful.
I cannot sit still, I need to move and make the most of my life
whilst I can.
Nothing can stop me until the bad news arrives and puts me back
into that dark place, and everything starts all over again.

Megan King (14)
Wymondham High School

Rich And Poor

As I wander down the street
I stare enviously at the big houses,
Only luckier people than me
Could afford.

I wish I could own
The big house, the wonderful car,
The posh clothes.
All I have is rags
And a blanket on the ground.

It seems as if the sun shines on them,
Day after day,
But the dark, gloomy rain cloud
Follows me everywhere.

As I slowly drift off into a sleep
Leaning against a couple of dustbins,
I dream about living in a house
Just like the ones I saw today.

I wonder what it would be like,
Just to have a house
Somewhere warm to go each night,

If only I was rich.

Emma Knivett (14)
Wymondham High School

A Place Where The Sun Shone

Like Matilda, she was captured by words that flowed down the page.
It sent her to a place, where all her suffering
and the darkness that plagued her
disappeared into the glowing light of her vivid imagination.
In this magical Narnia, where the sun shone on the horizon,
she was at peace.
The birds danced about the treetops,
while the water gently trickled over silky smooth rocks.
Here, in her imagination, the characters from the book
stepped out from the pages.
She was no longer alone.
But then the story ended and the characters faded.
Back to reality she came.
Back to the dreary, wet Monday evening,
back to the greyness of her boring life.

Hannah Lane (14)
Wymondham High School